Prayer Everywhere

THE SPIRITUAL LIFE MADE SIMPLE

Fr. Gary Caster

franciscan
media
Cincinnati, Ohio

Cover and book design by Mark Sullivan

ISBN 978-1-63253-251-0

Published by Franciscan Media
28 W. Liberty St.
Cincinnati, OH 45202
www.FranciscanMedia.org

Printed in the United States of America.
Printed on acid-free paper.

19 20 21 22 5 4 3 2

For all the students I have had the privilege of serving.

Contents

Foreword

I HAVE HEARD FATHER CASTER preach many, many times. He is, quite easily, one of the best homilists I have ever heard—he is authentic, engaging, funny, educational, and passionate. His homilies vary and yet, I have heard him say repeatedly that he really only has one: to tell people "Just let him love you." The first time I head Father say that he only has one homily, I didn't understand. I had heard him preach repeatedly, and it seemed to me that not once had Father recycled ideas. Then the longer I knew Father (twenty years now), the more I understood what he meant. His priestly goal, always, and in everything, is to encourage people to open their hearts to God.

He encourages people to do this because he has done it himself, and it has a daily impact on his life. Father Caster is one of the only people I have known to have complete, total, and utter confidence in God. He does not question God. He knows Christ and he knows him crucified. He does not doubt the effect of the Holy Spirit in his life. He does not waver in God's endless mercy. He doesn't treat God like a vending machine, making endless requests. He doesn't turn on God during hard times in life. He is resolute in the ways God has been present in his life, and nothing anyone says or does will cause him to question his faith in God. It is because of this surety that Father Caster can speak so confidently to us about developing our own spiritual life.

This confidence in God is precisely the thing that draws so many people to Father Caster and his life stories. This very book in fact was inspired by others campaigning on social media that Father share his life journey to the priesthood. Father initially discounted the idea, but like his good friend, the Little Flower, Father needed others to affirm his wonderfully unique, holy, unwavering, and joyful relationship with Christ. (St. Thérèse of Lisieux's sister prompted her to write her autobiography, now known as *Story of a Soul*.) Father Caster needed the encouragement of loved ones to say, "Your story matters, and the world will be a better place should others have access to it." In so many ways, those who were a part of the social media post that day were begging, "Please, help us to understand, give us insight into how God works in your life. We see that he makes a difference in you and how you live life and how you love others. Tell us more."

When friends started campaigning for Father Caster to write a book about his life's catchphrase, "Just let him love you," people were asking Father to share some of the deepest parts of his heart. The risk of his being vulnerable was not considered.

We are so quick to volunteer another to share of themselves, to let us hear their story, to know the inner workings of how their heart and mind operate, and yet we are so very reserved to do the same. How many times in a conversation when someone has shared an intimate part of themselves have you also wanted to share part of your story, only to hold back, not knowing how they might interpret what you are saying or knowing they might misunderstand where you were coming from or calculating if you are choosing the right words. It is hard to be vulnerable with people you know. It is hard to take risks with people you do not know. It is hard to reveal yourself to people who might misunderstand. It is hard to reveal your heart to people who might be unkind to you. It is hard to bare yourself to people who see the world differently than you. It is hard to be vulnerable. Being truly who you are, and sharing that with others, is terrifying, really.

Then, there is Jesus. There is no one more vulnerable. Think about the risk that God took coming to us as a tiny infant. Think about how he revealed himself with the woman at the well and when he corrected the Pharisees about their misunderstandings of God the Father. Consider his vulnerability in weeping openly at the death of his friend Lazarus or in washing the feet of the apostles or when he hung on the cross.

Think of the vulnerability of the saints. Catherine of Siena made herself vulnerable every time that she received communion. She would fall into a state of ecstasy, causing paralysis of her body. Eventually, fellow parishioners tossed her out on the stairs of the church. Can you imagine the talk of the town? "She's so overdramatic and always looking for attention," they might have said. Catherine could have simply chosen not to receive communion.

What about Thérèse of Lisieux, who approached her parish priest, begging that he allow her to receive her first Holy

Communion at an age before all of her peers. Can you imagine also the potential ridicule her parents might have dealt with? From the priest? From other parishioners? "Who does she think she is to be above the guidelines that are in place for everyone?"

Think about John Paul II. At the end of his life, he struggled to sit upright, speak clearly, or to be able to lift his arms to give a blessing. Can you imagine the talk of newscasters and national leaders? "He is too old to be a good shepherd for the Church," they said.

What you have before you in this book is true vulnerability. Father Caster himself has very little to gain from sharing his life of faith with us. This book is a piece of his heart put out there for the world to see. (If it were me writing the book, I would have to keep repeating John Paul II's exhortation, "Be not afraid!") However, because Father lives authentically, because he responds to the movement of the Holy Spirit, and because he cannot be silent about the one true living God, he shares of himself. He shares in the hope that it will draw you into knowing the one who loves with no bounds. He shares in the hope that you will know the one who forgives and calls us back to himself. He shares in the hope that you will come to know the heart of God. He hopes that the encounter you have with Christ will stir up in you an insatiable desire to be vulnerable yourself.

Therefore, before delving into what is sure to be an incredible story of God's work in one man's life, we must never forget that our own journey with God is just as incredible. It matters just as much. Our story too needs telling. Maybe not written down in a book, but shared in our parish hall, at school pickup, in our work places, when we are out to dinner to with friends, and in every seemingly ordinary moment of our day. Your relationship with Jesus is one of a kind because you are one of a kind. Nevertheless, that one of a kind story is a story that might encourage someone else to know Jesus better. Let us go out into the world and just let him love us. That love will change the world.

—Jennifer Sagel

Preface

AT THE DINNER MY PARENTS hosted on the evening following my ordination to the Catholic priesthood, my older brother began his toast in the following way: "My brother Gary had a perfect hate-hate relationship with the seminary: he hated them and they hated him." Yet there I was, a newly ordained minister of the Gospel.

In fairness to my brother, the fact that I had attended five seminaries in seven and a half years was not the only reason he thought this way about my journey to the altar. It was also my own restlessness to be ordained and my critical running commentary on the seminaries I attended. The years I spent in formation were not the best in the history of the Catholic Church.

Each of the seminaries I attended had problems, some worse than others. For example, at one "house of formation," one female faculty member was both a professed religious and self-avowed witch. At another, two priests were in active sexual relationships with male students. Another seminary I attended forbade Eucharistic Adoration and frowned upon popular devotions such as the rosary. At morning and evening prayer, the faculty often replaced Scripture readings with excerpts from the *New York Times* or *Washington Post* or obscure poems chosen by the lector. Some men lived in apartments and commuted to their classes and formation activities.

A religious sister led the first "retreat" I attended during my second year in formation. Before the retreat began, she placed numerous crystals on a table and asked us to "feel" which one spoke to us. She expected us to place our personal crystal on the altar during the offertory. I thought the entire thing was, well, crazy.

This retreat took place at the motherhouse of a religious community of women where the older and infirm sisters were kept in seclusion upstairs and not allowed contact with us. They would, however, sneak into the choir loft and toss us notes written on scraps of paper that said, "Pray for us," and, "Help us!"

One of the more bizarre moments from these particular years was receiving the encouragement to "grow beyond the Eucharist." While I am still not entirely sure what that means, at the time, I pretended to take the critique seriously. I therefore asked the faculty if they might recommend books that could help guide me toward this goal. At this same meeting, the faculty told me that I did not dress in an age-appropriate manner. (I was twenty-five!) Instead of explaining to them that I had given away everything I owned before entering the seminary, that my six items of clothes were all I had, that my parents were not financially supporting me, and that I literally had not a penny to my name, I respectfully asked their advice and assured them my appearance would change.

When I shared their concern with my spiritual director (a priest not affiliated with the seminary), we had a great laugh trying to figure out just what they meant. Some days later, my spiritual director took me to Lord & Taylor and bought me an assortment of Haggar slacks and a supply of long-sleeve dress shirts. For the rest of my time at this seminary, I was always—in my mind—terribly overdressed! Not to mention, I missed my Levi's 501 blue jeans, which is exactly what I was wearing the day I meet Mother Teresa, who never said a word about the appropriateness of my attire. The picture of us sits on my desk to this day.

Just for the record, the joke was actually on all of these well-intentioned men and women. Jesus did tell us to be as clever as serpents and as innocent as doves, and what the formation team did not realize is that I would have worn burlap if it meant becoming a priest. My sole purpose in being there was to learn what I needed in order to serve as a priest and grow closer to Christ. Compared to my years living and working in Hollywood, the seminary was at best a low-budget carnival or a cheap B-movie.

When asked to leave this particular house of the macabre, the priest serving as rector told me, "I will personally see to it that you are never ordained!"

Can you imagine the arrogance? I rolled my eyes and told him to give it his best shot. I know, not a very mature response.

Some years later, while vesting to concelebrate Mass at the Basilica Shrine of the Immaculate Conception, I happened to run into the man that threatened to prevent my ordination. I walked right up to him and said, "Well Larry, I guess we both know you failed!" Yes, I have confessed my smarmy, infantile behavior.

You see, my faith is extremely simple. I was fortunate to be raised by a mother who showed me how easy it was to be a follower of Christ. I was not raised to be afraid of God or spend my time trying to prove myself to him. Rather, I was encouraged to let him love me, or as Pope Emeritus Benedict XVI has famously said, "lavish his love" upon me.

I credit my mother's influence on my spiritual formation with opening me to a profound encounter with Jesus. This took place on a Thursday afternoon in June when I was nine years old, and changed the way I thought about others and myself and the way I thought about the world around me. This encounter did not make me perfect or holy. It simply convicted me of God's love for me. This truth is the rock foundation upon which I have built my life. (And the winds and floods of seminary formation were not able to wash it away.)

Thanks to my mother, I do not take very kindly to people trying to assess whether or not and to what extent I know the Lord or am truly contrite, appropriately humble, or authentically orthodox. I met Jesus on that Thursday afternoon, and I have been getting to know him better ever since. To this day, he still finds me adorable (obviously not in the sense of worship) and wants what is best for me. Jesus is exceedingly patient with me. I know I make him smile, and at times, I am sure he rolls his eyes.

Because of the graced experience I had at age nine, I have objected to people who think they have control over me or my relationship with God. I still do not. This disposition did not always sit well with the priests and religious sisters I met on my journey to the altar. In fact, one much-loved spiritual director continually tried to convince me to leave. One evening, he found me late at night in the Blessed Sacrament Chapel of the College sitting before the tabernacle crying.

When he asked why, I told him, "Because I love him."

He shook his head from side to side and, sighing, asked, "What does that even mean?"

I looked at him through my teary eyes and in a disgusted tone replied, "If I have to explain it to you, maybe you should consider leaving." (I have confessed this too.)

Remember, I did not say my encounter with Jesus perfected me; I am still running the race and "working out my salvation with fear and trembling" (see Philippians 2:12)

Looking back, I realize there was a better way to explain to Father Director the reason for my tears of joy. I should have shared with him how my mother taught me that I am the only person that stands in the way of my relationship with Christ. That no one and nothing can prevent me from becoming the person God created me to be, except me! I should have explained that Christ was letting me know that I truly do love him. How this was his gift to me, a grace I needed in order to continue. What I never shared with the house spiritual director, and probably should have, was my reason for going to the chapel: to tell Jesus that I was finished, that I could not take the craziness anymore, and that I was leaving. For years, I knew of and never doubted Jesus's love for me, but that night Jesus was letting me know and experience interiorly my love for him. It is another unrepeatable experience that changed my life.

At every seminary I attended, I tried to explain to those responsible for my formation that if Jesus wanted me to be a priest, I would become one. In spite of the many perversions and distortions of my seven and half years in formation, the single greatest problem during all that time was always me and not the seminary. Then as now, my life needed to change in so many ways. Although I was frequently frustrated and often confused by what transpired, I was never at war with the seminary. I did not try to change it or make it more orthodox. I was always at war with Gary. I still do battle with Gary to this day.

When I entered the seminary, it was the second time I had applied. I promised God that if I were accepted, I would spend the time allowing him to change my life and teach me everything I needed to know to serve him and his people. This instilled within me a strong sense of confidence. I believed then and now that Jesus will be faithful to his word to complete the good work he began in me on that Thursday long ago. Unfortunately, my confidence in Christ was most often mistaken to be arrogance (and thus another reason for my brother's toast).

Being accepted into formation convinced me that I was doing exactly what Jesus wanted me to do. I had wanted to be a priest since I was in the second grade. I applied during my senior year of high school and was rejected without any explanation. Nevertheless, the desire to serve the Lord as a priest never waned. I went away to college wondering, conflicted, and confused. I was absolutely sure the priesthood was God's plan for me. How could they have turned me away? Unfortunately, I did not have anyone that I felt could help me through this internal turmoil, so I just refused to accept that I was wrong. I talked with Jesus about it incessantly and wrote daily about my thoughts and feelings in a journal. Maybe this is the reason he gave me a second chance. Like the woman before the judge, I simply wore Jesus down.

Now what does any of this have to do with a book on the spiritual life? Good question. I think it is vitally important you know something about the man that wants to tell you how easy it is to live one. My confidence in Jesus and my firm conviction of his love for me guided me through the seminary, and today I am as confident, perhaps more so, than I ever was. Sadly, it continues to be mistaken as arrogance. No matter, I will always take St. Thomas Aquinas at his word. When asked about how to obtain salvation, he replied, "Will it!"

Regardless of my fragility, weakness, and sin, I personally expect to enter the gates of heaven with a band playing "When the Saints Go Marching In"! Not because of anything I can accomplish; I am weak, fickle, and, too much of the time, self-absorbed. Nevertheless, I rely on and accept God's promises, his mercy, goodness, and love. I want for me what God wants for me; in fact, I *will* what God has promised me. This lies at the heart of how I live my life with Christ and serve him as a priest. I hope at the end of this book that it might lie at the heart of your relationship with Christ and that for the rest of your life, you will just let him love you.

Introduction

SOME MONTHS BEFORE I WAS ordained, my bishop told me he planned to send me to teach at one of our Catholic high schools. The idea terrified me. I was not popular the first time around and imagined my new experience would be much the same. My bishop—ever patient with me—told me to trust his decision, be myself, and share with the students my relationship with Christ.

The first and most important thing I learned was how easy it was for students to spot a phony. They had little interest in a talking head, a know-it-all, an encyclopedia (which accurately describes my first semester). I was so excited about sharing with them the beauty of the Catholic faith and having them see it the way I did that I ended up caring more about the material than I did for them. Fortunately, a disgruntled young student had the courage to bring this to my attention. He openly challenged me to explain exactly how all this material affected my life. He did not want abstract concepts and interesting theories. His direct rebuke, "What difference does any of this make?" taught me a valuable lesson about the true nature of evangelization. Today this young man is an outstanding priest, an author, and an educator himself.

Since it is impossible for me to explain the difference a life of faith makes without describing how to live it, answering this young man's question provided me with an opportunity to describe what nourished and sustained my life with Christ. It was easy for me to talk about the real impact the Trinity, the Eucharist, the Scriptures, and so on, have on my daily life, and it generated great discussions. It was easy, therefore, to challenge them to do the same. I used to say to them, "The best possible experience of life comes from following Christ. I should know, because I have the best life of anyone I know! The only way to disprove me is to follow Christ and see whether or not I'm right." Everyone that has ever taken up my challenge is still following him. The question then is, "How do we follow him?"

Before setting down all that following Christ entails, I think there are a few things that need clarification, principles to keep in mind while you live out your life with Christ.

IT'S NOT THE THINGS YOU DO

The single greatest difficulty people face when following Christ is an effect of reducing one's spiritual life to one's religious practices. This is why many people leave the Catholic Church. They think that the pious, devotional, and obligatory things that comprise practicing the faith equate to having a life of faith. This is simply not true. The rosaries recited, the hours racked up before the Blessed Sacrament, all the Masses attended, chaplets prayed, and fasts obeyed do not necessarily indicate one is following Jesus. Many people do these things—all of them good things to do—because someone told them to. Fulfilling one's duties and obligations, while significant dimensions of any healthy relationship, is not in and of itself the relationship. Over time, many Catholics lose interest and fall away because they do not know this. God created us for himself, not for religious practices: "The Sabbath was made for man, not man for the Sabbath" (Mark 2:27).

Now, lest anyone accuse me of disparaging pious practices and religious obligations, hear me out. They are not and cannot be the heart of our spiritual lives. Christ has told us in his own words that he alone must be the rock foundation on which we build our lives. This can only happen if we have actually encountered him, as did the people that followed him in the Gospels. Once we have decided to leave everything to follow Christ, it becomes readily apparent that we need help in doing so. Thus, if we want to follow him, we must seek out and grab hold of those things that nourish and sustain us in doing so.

The organization of the Catholic Church is for just this purpose. The Scriptures preserved and handed down, the moral and social teachings which flow from them, and the sacramental life enlivened by the Holy Spirit, enable us to adhere to Christ as we follow him toward our destiny with the Father. Even during his public ministry, Jesus made it abundantly clear that we do not follow him as individuals alone; we follow him as companions. I cannot therefore experience fully my relationship with Christ in isolation from his body, the Church. It would be something like the big toe trying to get around by itself without the rest of the foot!

One of the many things I love about the Catholic Church is the refusal to mandate a one-size-fits-all approach to living our life with Christ. The Church simply sets before us a rich treasury of practices that enhance, encourage, enliven, and even embolden our life with Christ. While many are strongly encouraged because they prove so efficacious, the Church imposes none of them upon us. We do not have to ever pray the rosary or Chaplet of Divine Mercy, make a holy hour, pray the Divine Office, or have a devotion to Mary or a particular saint. While we must attend Mass on Sundays and holy days, fast and abstain with the Church (according to our age and health), receive the Eucharist once a year, go to confession if we are conscious of having committed a serious sin, and financially support the mission of the Church according to our means, we are never told what to do in between. This is incumbent upon each individual believer. In other words, it is up to each one of us, and I find this refreshing.

I cannot stress this point enough. Far too many people in trying to begin a spiritual life merely adopt the most popular spiritual practices or disciplines. Usually they take too much upon themselves, including things that do not actually nourish them. In the end, they fail, and this leads them to think poorly of themselves. Eventually they conclude God must also think poorly of them. This eventually leads to resentment.

This is one reason why I am glad I am not God. He does not tell us what to do and never thinks poorly of us for trying. He does not deserve our recriminations when the plans we set for ourselves do not come to fruition. Instead of being angry at failure, we should simply try again, but this time with a plan that is reasonable and workable.

After high school, my younger sister burned rubber leaving the Catholic Church. She wanted to get as far away as possible. Years later, married with two children, she called one day asking how to go about having a spiritual life. I told her to do one thing for ten days. When I told her what it was (I will tell you soon enough), she was upset with me. She had expected me to foist upon her all sorts of activities. I told her to do this one thing and not to call me for ten days. Only when time was up would we talk about what to do next. She was not happy. Two days later, she called. I did not take her call. She tried again on the third, but I did not take her call. Finally, she waited until the ten days were up, and I took the call. She was excited and amazed that something so incredibly easy had already begun to change her life. When she died at age thirty-six, she was good friends with Jesus and extremely close with his mother.

It's Not a Means to an End

The second most common reason for failure in the spiritual life lies in treating it as a means to an end. No one should undertake a substantive life of prayer and devotion thinking it will make them holy, eradicate all suffering, or assure a comfortable, successful life. In no way is this what following Christ entails. This is just an attempt at gaming God, and it treats prayer as a form of magic. Thinking that God must do certain things for me because of what I do for God is an absolute and egregious blasphemy! God does not bend to my will or yours; as followers of Christ, we are supposed to bend to his. God is never bound by what we do, even when done out of love for him. We should undertake the things we do for God simply because we must, period. I spend time with Jesus each day not because of how it makes me feel (sometimes I really do not feel like it) or because I promised the Church I would. I do it because I cannot live without it, and in fact, I could not get out of bed if I did not.

Perhaps there are other motivations for embracing each new day, but the only one that works for me is Jesus.

Those who undertake to follow Christ must never lose sight of the fact that the spiritual life is an end in and of itself. The spiritual practices I undertake as I adhere to Christ are all things that I must do. Without them, I would be unable to continue progressing with him on my journey to everlasting life. I should pray the rosary because I have found in the rhythm and pattern of the repeated prayers the space I need to reflect upon the life of the one I follow. If I pray the Chaplet of Divine Mercy, it should flow from a desire to penetrate more deeply the sacrificial offering of Christ's passion and death. The awareness of my need to be with the Lord should compel me to sit before him, present in the Blessed Sacrament.

The entire pattern of my life of prayer should be rooted in the recognition that I cannot live my life with Christ otherwise. If any of the things that make up my spiritual practices are done out of a hope for gaining something, then I should immediately stop doing them! Our Lady does not care how many rosaries one says or even if one says it at all. However, she does care about the extent to which we are evermore opening our hearts to her Son. Jesus remains the focus and foundation of her eternal life; thus, she continues to serve him by encouraging us to do the same.

Jesus offers his most detailed description of judgment in Matthew 25:31–46. He does not say to those on his right, "Come, you who are blessed by my Father, for you spent six million hours before me, never missed a Sunday Mass, prayed fifteen million rosaries, read your Bible every day, and went regularly to confession. Now enjoy the place prepared for you from the foundation of the world." Jesus makes no mention of spiritual practices, devotional activities, or scriptural acumen. He does, however, make mention of the way in which those on his right not only recognized their neighbor's needs but, more importantly, responded. Of course, I would argue that it is unlikely we could be responsive in the way Jesus describes unless our lives were rooted in his. Pious and devotional practices do not make us responsive; they keep us firmly rooted in the Lord and his goodness. This, in turn, informs the way we see God, ourselves, others, and the world around us.

It should come as no surprise, then, that a spiritual life is not the way to get to heaven. Jesus alone is the Way. In order to follow him on this way, we need to be attentive to the one we are following. The spiritual life is more accurately a description of the *way* we follow than it is a guarantee that we are, in fact, following.

YOU ARE YOUR SPIRITUAL LIFE

This is perhaps the most important of all the points I want to make before we begin. What does it mean to say that one is one's spiritual life? It means that every aspect of my life flows from and thereby expresses my relationship with Christ (or should). My spiritual life is not only the moments I am conscious of God or talking with him in personal or communal prayer. Rather, every waking moment constitutes my following of Christ. Eating, drinking, sleeping, working, playing, thinking, resting... every human activity and endeavor, no matter how grand or seemingly insignificant, should be rooted in the relationship I have with Jesus. My life with Christ had better be my life, or essentially, I do not have a life with Christ.

For those born in the Western world, especially in the United States, this can be difficult to understand. We have a tendency to compartmentalize our lives, to see the different things we do merely as activities, each one unconnected from the others and having its own proper end. We have thereby succeeded in reducing religious practices and spirituality to the innocuous status of just another activity, one possibility among many others, equally valid as all the rest.

As a result, we try to balance the amount of time we give to the different things we do. In truth, however, if we gave the right kind of time to nourishing our relationship with Jesus, we would not waste so much time trying to ensure that the other things we do are as meaningful as possible. Once our focus, our gaze, and our recourse is solely Jesus, the other aspects of our lives are less burdensome, more productive, and less likely to determine how we value ourselves.

Treating our relationship with Christ as just another activity also inhibits the action of the Holy Spirit and thus impedes the transformation of our minds and hearts. The Lord cannot be at work in me if I am only allowing him the time I spend doing pious or prayerful things. I must open the whole of my life to Christ and intentionally make him a vital part of everything I do. I used to tell my high school students to invite Jesus to come with them to the class they hated most.

"Make him sit there with you," I would say. "Since Jesus cares about you and your life, he certainly won't mind enduring class with you."

The students that tried this, even if for no other reason than to test it out, found that it did affect their time in the classroom.

Many of them started looking forward to these classes because they knew they could share with Jesus what they did not like—while it was happening. One young woman would journal her comments to Jesus and discovered that, in doing so, she was also taking notes on the subject at hand. I personally like to bring Jesus to the meetings I know are the least productive. It helps with patience since I know he is right there next to me.

Now I imagine this might sound a tad bit silly, but remember, Jesus does say, "Behold I stand at the door and knock. If anyone hears my voice and opens the door, then I will enter" (see Revelation 3:20). Jesus wants access to every facet of our lives. He wants in. So I say, "Kick that door down!" Let Jesus accompany you everywhere you go, the mall, the grocery store, the office, the laundry room...everywhere! There is no place in your life that Jesus is not knocking and calling, "Let me in." This same man invites his disciples to have breakfast with him. Nothing we do is insignificant or unimportant to the Savior of the world. He said he is with us until the end of the ages, and I choose to take him at his word. After all, he is God.

I have a friend who takes Jesus or a particular saint to Walmart with her, a place she does not enjoy going. Now she finds herself more patient when she is there and less stressed when she is finished. Sometimes she even enjoys her outings because she knows she is not alone. Talking with a saintly friend or the Son of God while you shop is a great way to go shopping. It is also a great way to do the dishes, iron, play a sport, take a walk, change diapers, and yes, make love with your spouse. (The Lord is not only the author of the human body, but also the one who elevated marriage to the status of a sacrament.)

For those who think Jesus has better things to do, consider this: You are the most important work that Jesus is up to, so why not let him be at work in you? Years ago, I had the privilege of meeting a young couple in Belgium that had a prayer corner in their bedroom at which they would kneel to pray before... you get the picture.

Once we realize that Jesus came to save the entire human person and not just the soul, so much of the worry, stress, and burdens we heap upon ourselves dissipate. Each one of us is an embodied soul. It still confounds me how many devout believers forget this truth of the faith. I will be human for all eternity, my body glorified like Jesus's own body. So I say, why wait? Instead, why not do what St. Paul suggests in First Corinthians 6:20, and glorify God with our bodies right now? The easiest way to do this is by inviting Christ to share in the whole of my bodily existence.

This may take some getting used to, as we have a tendency to think that Jesus is only interested in spiritual things. This way of thinking, however, easily lends itself to heresy. One of the earliest is by a man that refused to accept that Jesus went to the bathroom! He just could not handle the Son of God being fully human. This tendency persists today. The best way to remain fully orthodox is by sharing the whole of our human lives with the one who wants to elevate them to the status of the divine. I can tell you with absolute certainty that Jesus really enjoys that I let him in on everything I do. Not one of us could possibly bore Jesus.

CHAPTER ONE

———∞∞∞———

Getting Started

"Just so, your light must shine before others, that they
may see your good deeds and glorify your heavenly
Father." (MATTHEW 5:16)

EACH OF US KNOWS THAT the strongest and most vibrant relationships are those sustained by good, healthy habits. We know
too that the most meaningful relationships develop over time,
even if begun all at once through unexpected encounters and
random circumstances.

For some mysterious reason, we seem to forget this when it
comes to our spiritual lives. Instead, we tend to want to jump
right in by heaping upon ourselves all sorts of spiritual practices
and rigorous disciplines. Thus, we overwhelm ourselves with
things we cannot possibly absorb into the fabric of our lives and
thereby lie crumpled beneath the weight of the burdens we have
heaped upon ourselves. This is precisely the reason so many
of us end up feeling like failures and concluding we are simply
incapable of praying and growing closer to God. Once again, I
feel it is important to stress that, unchecked, these feelings too

often lead to resentment against God and those who seem to be able to follow him.

At such times, I always feel sorry for God. He does not deserve to be derided for the outlandish practices we construct in an attempt to prove worthy of his love or draw closer to him. I think in the face of the resentments we may harbor, he says, "Wait a minute! I did not tell you to do all those things you wanted to do, to punch a holy hour time clock, or put on a prayer Fitbit. You chose all of that, so do not blame me. All I've ever wanted is you!"

Perhaps you have felt crushed by the burdens you have placed upon yourself. Maybe you resent not living up to what you think you should be doing when it comes to prayer and having a spiritual life. Well, I have good news for you. Those days are over! You can have a spiritual life. You can truly live your life through, with, and in Christ!

It begins with remembering that God created you for himself. Thus, having a relationship with him should not be fraught with overwhelming difficulties. Within the recesses of every human heart is a longing that only God can satisfy. True, our relationship with God does not happen all at once. It needs to develop in the same way as with our parents, siblings, and spouses, and others with whom we long to be friends. Like all the relationships that genuinely matter, the effort we put into them is worth it and certainly not a burden.

Coming to know God takes time, and it should. After all, it is supposed to last for all eternity. When it comes to our relationship with God, we should be in it for the long haul. So do not rush it, and do not push yourself to unrealistic extremes. Settle in and remind yourself frequently and often that this is forever. So take a breath and continue on—as my sister would tell you from heaven—slow and steady.

Now I realize that what I have said might be upsetting for the more theologically minded. You may be saying to yourself, "What about concupiscence and the fact we are sinners!" While I will address the popular preoccupation with sin later on, for now I think it is important for you to know that concupiscence has not put to death our innate desire for God. Our hearts are restless and can be fickle (and boy, do I know it!), but nonetheless, they yearn for God—"like a deer for running streams" (see Psalm 42). Concupiscence is merely a residue of original sin that exists within each one of us, even after baptism. It is the tension we experience between wanting to do what we want as opposed to doing that which we ought to do. We should not, however, overdramatize it or give it any more attention than it deserves. Yes, there are certainly going to be times when I am going to want to do what I want and may even follow through with it. However, this does not mean my heart stops yearning for God. It just means I am weak, fragile, vulnerable, and sometimes selfish.

The tension that exists within each one of us is not necessarily bad and is not in and of itself sinful. Like our human emotions, the tension concupiscence causes is neutral. Those who play stringed instruments know the importance of tension with respect to producing a desired note. Those who are skilled with a bow and arrow (by the way, in Hebrew the word *sin* comes from archery) understand the importance of having the correct amount of tension in order to hit the target. Some of the greatest music our lives play before the Lord flows from our willingness to strike the right chord even when we do not really want to. Hitting the bull's-eye in terms of living our humanity rightly also rests upon the right amount of tension. Imagine the music your life and mine can make before the Lord. I think this a much more positive way to think about those moments that seem to test us.

As you prepare to live more intentionally your life with Christ, make a mental note (or an actual one) to remind yourself as often as needed that what you are about corresponds exactly to how you have been created. Getting started is as easy as saying to yourself—and meaning it—"This alone is the fullness of life, and I want it!" Remember, those that asked Jesus for something received what they asked for, so be bold!

CHAPTER TWO

Framing Your Day

NOW IT IS TIME TO get going. As I mentioned earlier, when my younger sister called and asked me how to go about having a spiritual life, I told her to do one thing only for ten days. The reason is simple. I wanted her to learn how important it is to frame the day before it gets underway. I am constantly surprised that people find this such a remarkable breakthrough. After all, athletes, performers, business people, and so many others know how important it is to get psyched up, that is, mentally prepared for competition and performances. Yet so many people fail to do this with respect to their daily lives with God! I guarantee that if you begin doing what I recommend on a daily basis, your lives will change. In fact, I defy anyone to prove me wrong.

You do not need to take my insignificant word for it either. When in September of 1986 I met and began a friendship with St. Teresa of Calcutta, she was the one that suggested a simple morning practice that has taught me the value of framing each day. She told me that every morning when I wake up, I should say aloud, "Good morning, Jesus!" It is something she did, but with the added words, "Come walk the earth in me."

I must confess that, at the time, I thought it was somewhat silly for a man to do this, but I figured since she was a living saint, there could be no harm in trying. The first few days did seem a bit strange even though I had my own room and no one heard me. Yet it was not long before I recognized the impact this common greeting was having on me. Long before I went to prayer or made my holy hour, my mind already was centered on the Lord. I was conscious of Jesus while I went through the normal activities to start my day, making my bed, showering, shaving, brushing my teeth.

It was not very long before I expanded the litany with which I begin my day, and it is something I suggest to those that ask me for spiritual direction. You will no doubt find your own morning offering, but here are the five things I say each morning.

"GOOD MORNING, JESUS!"

I am glad I listened to a saint. A simple greeting can make all the difference in how the day unfolds. One of the greatest difficulties people experience in terms of a relationship with God has to do with feeling disconnected. They struggle to find just the right activity to overcome the distance and reconnect with God. What they fail to remember is that the humanity of Jesus is the way God used to connect with us. Jesus is not far away in some unapproachable heaven; he is not on an extended vacation. He is still here, still present, still approachable, still the Way that connects us with the Father. We need to remind ourselves of this every day. (Sometimes I need to do this every hour of every day!)

Greeting Jesus is a natural and human way of staying connected because greetings are the most common way we connect with others and affirm our shared humanity. They are so much more than polite practices or expressions of civility. They ground us. This is the reason Jesus greets people after his resurrection. His "Peace be with you" is not a grand gesture with deep theological significance. It is the way people of his time greeted one another. It was the same as saying, "good evening" or "good afternoon." It is much the same as saying, "Come have breakfast." Jesus greets his followers as a natural means of connecting his glorified humanity with their humanity, just as he had done throughout his ministry. By grounding his new state of being, he prevents his glorified body from becoming for them and for us an unapproachable spectacle. No wonder he was preoccupied with meals. No wonder he let Thomas touch him.

By greeting the Lord each morning, we begin the day by connecting our life with the life of the incarnate Christ. We tether his life with our own by reminding ourselves of the relationship that matters most to us.

"I GIVE YOU PERMISSION TODAY TO SPOIL ME WITH YOUR LOVE."
My favorite saint is Thérèse of Lisieux, "The Little Flower" (the saint from whom Mother Teresa took her religious name). I have been friends with the Little Flower since the fourth grade. Her way of talking about the faith and her understanding of God resonated with my own experience of faith formed so well by my mother. For St. Thérèse, God was not mean, angry, and ready to cast us all into hell. God was a font and source of love. He was not expecting us to prove our love to him because his Son had proved his love for us on the cross. At a young age, I learned from St. Thérèse that the one thing God expected most from me was to let him love me.

One of the most grave and disturbing things I have encountered as a priest is the number of people that do not believe God loves them. Far too many people think that they must first prove their love to God before God will extend himself to them. Every time I meet people shocked by the truth that God loves them, it breaks my priestly heart. How could they not know that God loves us in his Son, even while we were yet (and are still) sinners?

I was therefore so grateful when Benedict XVI released his first encyclical (on my birthday no less) *Deus Caritas Est*. It begins with the powerful and reassuring words, "I wish in my first Encyclical to speak of the love which God lavishes upon us and which we in turn must share with others" (1). At last, I had the backing of someone with great stature. It would no longer simply be my word about God lavishing his love upon us, but that of the ultimate Catholic authority.

There is however something that must follow accepting this truth of our Catholic faith. We must expect—demand—God to do so each day. This is not as brash as it may sound when you consider that everyone that comes to Jesus demanding something from him—sight, wholeness, hearing, life—receives what they ask for. Even one of the criminals condemned to die alongside him receives more than what he asks for. He gets paradise!

God is love. This means that love is not merely an activity, sentiment, or feeling in God. It is not something that is on or off in God. God is always God. We can easily forget this, so I think it is extremely important to remind ourselves each day to let God be who he is. At any moment of my day, I can tell you how God is spoiling me with his love, and more than that, I am always expecting it and therefore have the eyes to see it. I can also tell you at any given moment what God is thinking. He is thinking of Gary! I am always on God's mind.

"I SAY YES TO ALL THAT IS EXPECTED OF ME TODAY AND YES TO ALL THAT'S UNEXPECTED."

Sometimes we do not wake up looking forward to the things we know we have to do, and even if we may be excited about all that the day holds, unexpected things can ruin our whole day.

When I recognized how true this was for me, I decided to do something about it. I knew there were many responsibilities expected of me because of my priestly life and my assignment, but not all of them were eagerly anticipated. Therefore, I began to say yes to them before the day got underway. That means later on, when facing these expectations, I could not complain about them; I had already told the Lord I would do them.

It was not very long before I found how freeing this was. It changed my state of mind with respect to some of the obligations that weren't the most exciting—like cleaning my bathroom, doing my laundry, ironing altar linens, vacuuming my rooms, and so on. (Yes, these are all expected tasks. I don't have a housekeeper or a cook). Faced with some of the less desirable duties of my life, I would undertake them, telling the Lord, "I know, I already said yes. I'm going to do it." Now, this does not mean I have come to enjoy some of these tasks (like cleaning my bathroom), it means I do not rebel against doing them. It has made them less of the burden my attitude had been making them out to be.

This change in perspective made me realize that much of the frustration and aggravation of any given day resulted from unexpected demands. Why rebel against them, when all I had to do was begin my day by telling the Lord, "I'm saying yes to all the unexpected demands on me today." Talk about freedom! Instead of being upset, I now anticipate what the unexpected demands might be. In this way, I put Satan in his place. Satan cannot frustrate or aggravate me, nor can he take away the peace that Christ has given me. Think of all the unexpected things that can ruin your whole good day—flat tires; sick, crying, or sleepless children; another demand on your time. Why let them define you or your disposition? I have found that beginning my day by saying yes prevents the unexpected from undoing me—most of the time. (Confession: I am still having some intermittent difficulty with unexpected travel problems, but with the help of the Spirit, I am making progress).

"I EXPECT YOU TO PUNCTUATE MY DAY WITH SIGNS OF YOUR PRESENCE." I say this each morning, and I put my whole self into it. I could not survive a day without the presence of the Lord, so I begin each day clearing the scales from my eyes and the noise from my ears. Jesus told his followers they must have eyes to see and ears to hear, so I think it is important that we begin each day prepared to see how he will manifest himself to us and be open to hearing his voice.

Jesus longs to fill our lives with the concrete experience of his abiding presence. He came into the world so that we might experience fullness of life now. Seated at the right hand of the Father, Jesus through the Spirit fulfills his promise. He has not left us orphaned or alone. We have only to be attentive to and expectant of the host of ways throughout the day in which he affirms that we are his. Despite the clutter, noise, and demands of daily life, Jesus remains present in the midst of it all. In the ordinary and expected demands of daily life, Jesus has chosen to pitch his tent and dwell with us. While it is understandable that we can and do lose sight of him, it is not because he is absent or disinterested. The omnipresent God is always present in his Son, encouraging, assisting, and directing us in all our undertakings.

In the words of the apostle John, we are God's children now! Thus, wherever we are and whatever we are doing, God is with us in his Son. I truly appreciate the ways in which the accounts of the resurrection appearances in the Gospel beautifully and powerfully underscore this point. Jesus does not reveal himself in bold, dramatic fashion, with special effects that would be fitting for the Son of God raised in splendor. Rather he simply is present wherever his followers find themselves, like a locked room, on a road outside of town, in a cemetery, on the shores of the sea. Although the followers of Christ were sad, frightened, confused, and forlorn, Jesus cares so much about them that he shows himself attentive to everything they are experiencing because of his death on the cross. He is with them where they are, and that remains true for us today.

If you ever wonder where God is, I have good news for you, he is right where you are. The easiest way not to lose sight of this for me is to begin my day reminding myself of this truth of the faith. I do so by telling Jesus what I expect. At any given moment of my day, I can recount exactly how Jesus has been present to me, punctuating my life with the grace of his presence. In fact, just saying his name brings calmness and clarity to every difficult situation.

"THANK YOU!"

There is no better way to conclude the framing of our day than by saying, "Thank you." Students often ask me what I am thankful for. I tell them I do not have a long list of the incredible things God has accomplished in my life, but simply that he has not yet given up on me. I know that God is with me for the long (or short) haul of my life, all the way through eternity. Through his commitment to me personally, I still want to serve him, however imperfectly, I still want to know him better, and I still long for his love to take possession of me. His persistent care of me, his unyielding commitment to me and to the ins and outs of my life, and his uplifting encouragement in the face of my repeated failings and boneheaded mistakes is reason enough for me to be thankful. Even if I do not enter heaven with the band playing my song, I will be eternally grateful for his love. In addition, I am thankful for taste buds. I really know God loves me when I eat.

CHAPTER THREE

Prayer

Train yourself for devotion, for, while physical training is of limited value, devotion is valuable in every respect, since it holds a promise of life both for the present and for the future. (1 TIMOTHY 4:7–8)

WHAT I WANT TO SHARE with you now is by no means a comprehensive, exhaustive treatise on prayer. That would be a near impossible task. Instead, I hope to offer some necessary insights into how it is that we limited, created realities can reach beyond ourselves to the source of all that is. That is in fact what we aim to do when we pray.

Prayer is almost as much a mystery as God. Prayer always seems to be more than the words we use to describe it or the ways in which we understand it. Prayer is as old as the human family, stretching all the way back to the fall of Adam and Eve. Prior to disobeying God, our first parents lived in friendship with him. The intimacy they shared precluded the need for prayer.

Their sin, however, produced a chasm between themselves and God. Because God created them to share his life, the desire for him not only remained, it also intensified. St. Augustine describes this as a restlessness within the human heart that can only be satisfied by resting in God. We can say, therefore, with a fair degree of certainty that prayer is the action that enables communication between that which is human and that which is divine. Prayer is the means by which human beings seek to access and experience God.

Notice I did not say prayer is the words we use to communicate with the divine. While prayer often consists of words, because we do have something to say, we praise God, we beg and bargain with God, we appeal to and pester God, and of course, we give thanks to God. Although speech may be the most common characteristic of prayer, prayer is so much more than speech alone. St. Thérèse of Lisieux, described prayer as "a surge of the heart; it is a simple look turned toward heaven, it is a cry of recognition and of love, embracing both trial and joy" (*Autobiography of a Soul*). Thérèse understood that prayer is a unique kind of activity that expresses the height and depth and breadth of being. She knew that, above all, it was a response to the transcendent. St. Thérèse wisely understood that prayer does not begin in us. Prayer is always a response to an invitation that initiates in the God that created us in his image and likeness.

As long as human beings have existed, we have sought ways of communing with the divine. This stretches back much further than the moment when God reached out in friendship to Abraham. For most of human history, we have accepted as an obvious fact that we are not the source of our existence, let alone the source of the created universe. Thus, from our earliest days we have sought ways of explaining the unknown and controlling the forces of nature. The most nascent, emergent, and initial forms of prayer found in ancient tribal societies demonstrate an innate need to assuage the restlessness caused by original sin. Prayer did not suddenly emerge with the election of Abraham and the people of Israel; it greatly matured. We can rightly describe the history of the human family as the story of humanity in search of reunion with God.

This search for reunion, friendship, or intimacy with the divine necessarily changed over time. Primitive forms of prayer, which had magical and mythical elements, evolved as we better understood the world around us and reflected upon the meaning of being human. Asking the big questions of origin, meaning, and purpose shaped our efforts at calming the innate restlessness of the human heart. Yet it was not enough.

In the midst of the growth and development of the human family, something remarkable takes place: God boldly reaches out! In calling out to Abraham, God takes the initiative of preparing for us a way back to him. In Abraham, it is as if the entire human family says yes to God's offer of friendship. Abraham speaks on behalf of every human heart that has struggled to find a way back to God and heal the original wound of our first parents. This is similar to St. Augustine's description of the annunciation. He says that all creation held its breath anticipating Mary's response to the words of the angel Gabriel.

Prior to Abraham, however, God was not hiding from the human family. God remained always present, sustaining the world in being and tirelessly calling out in love to every human heart. Patiently, God was revealing himself to us through the created order, waiting for the "fullness of time" (Hebrews 1:1) when we would be able to speak to him as "one friend speaks to another" (Exodus 33:11). With great care, God watched over the human family, and through the election of Abraham, God reveals how he was acting in history through concrete conditions and circumstances. In the Old Testament, we learn that "prayer…is the relationship with God in historical events" (CCC 2568).

Revelation also teaches us that we live our lives between two great historical moments. The moment God calls out to our sinful parents, "Where are you?" (Genesis 3:9), and the moment Jesus says to the Father, "I have come to do your will" (Hebrews 10:7). Most of us Christians spend our lives somewhere between hiding from God and honestly trying to do his will. Prayer not only prevents us from cowering before God, it also strengthens us to continue saying yes to the Father. Prayer keeps us right where we need to be.

Jesus reveals this fundamental dimension of prayer throughout the whole of his life. From his parents, he learns to pray in his heart and with his people. As he grows, these habits of prayer receive an infusion from the hidden source of his being. His communion with the Father interpenetrates his growth and development and propels him toward the ministry for which he came. Thus, we see him praying before all the decisive events of salvation history, humbly entrusting his human will to the loving will of his Father. This is now for us the perfect model of prayer and ensures for us the way of confidence because, like Jesus, we know that the Father always hears us.

The knowledge of who we have become in Christ should

therefore infuse the prayer of our hearts, our devotional practices, and our prayers with the Christian community. We have become sons and daughters of the Father! His life united with our own should elevate and illuminate all our endeavors (including mopping floors, changing diapers, making our beds, taking out the trash, vacuuming, sitting through dull meetings.) The truth of being God's children now sets us free and ensures the full, vibrant experience of being human which Jesus came to give us. Prayer keeps our lives engaged with the life of the Father, the Son, and the Holy Spirit.

Without prayer, we run the risk of forgetting who we have become, and slowly we begin to feel as if God is distant and uninterested. Prayer also prevents us from hiding from God (like Adam), for through it, we place ourselves before the only one that can perfect us and transform our lives. Every prayer, whether spoken or not, alone or with others, is truly an opportunity to say to Lord, "Fill me with your life. Change me into the person you know me to be." Just by accepting God's invitation to be in his presence, we open ourselves to the infinite, giving the Spirit permission to act in the deepest recesses of our being. Moreover, we do so, as St. Thérèse has said, by the simple surge of our hearts to the one that saves us from ourselves. This alone should be reason to pray at all times!

Perhaps the most beautiful truth about prayer is that it is never really ours. We do not control its dimensions, its scope, or even its productivity. We may grab our rosary beads, drag ourselves to Mass, recite the psalms five times a day as we have promised, or pray the words of our favorite chaplet, but the impetus is always from the Holy Spirit. The Spirit uses the various forms of prayer by which we approach God in order to instruct, strengthen, and nourish us. The Spirit is the living water Jesus promised the Samaritan woman. Through the movement of the rosary beads, the rhythm of the liturgy, the familiarity of the psalms, and other modes of Christian prayer, we stir up the living water who, in turn, gathers all we long to say and need to say when presenting us to the Father.

Of course, none of this can happen if we are not in the habit of praying. Our hope of growing into the new creation we have become in Christ depends upon our life of prayer being something greater than the extemporaneous outpouring of interior impulses. Prayer must be for each follower of Christ a willed act, a determined response to the one who lovingly gave his life for us. Prayer cannot depend on human sentiment or human emotion. We must come to view our time of prayer as a life-sustaining necessity that prevents us from losing the salvation won for us by Christ. St. Alphonsus Liguori says, "Those who pray are certainly saved; those who do not pray are certainly damned" (CCC 2744).

For this reason, the Catechism describes prayer as a battle "against ourselves and against the wiles of the tempter who does all he can to turn man away from prayer, away from union with God" (CCC 2725). We must therefore be vigilant with respect to prayer, humble before the one who calls us. We must trust in the good purposes of God's will and persevere through love. Prayer and the Christian life are inseparable. Even the apostles recognized this, for they begged Jesus, "Teach us to pray" (Luke 11:1). If we are resolute in making time each day to be alone with the Lord, oh the things that he will teach and show us, oh the love that he will lavish upon us.

One last but very important point about prayer: The best time to pray is when we least feel like praying. After all, it is true that we do not always feel like going to Mass, sitting alone with the Lord, saying our prayers. In such moments, we should force ourselves to cry out to the Lord, to push through our feelings, misgivings, frustrations, and doubts. If you want to show the Lord how much you love him, deny how you are feeling, what you are thinking about your paltry efforts and halfhearted attempts, and be present to him.

I knew a seminarian who was home one summer and was in the habit of meeting with other seminarians to make a holy hour. One particular afternoon, that was the last thing he wanted to do. He went, largely because he did not want to admit to his brothers that he did not want to go.

He met the others at a local parish church and they all took a separate pew to be alone in prayer. He knelt down and told the Lord, "I really wish I could be doing something else. I am just mentally somewhere else, so I am just going to sit here until the hour is up. I'm sorry."

Well, time stretched out, and the minutes seemed like hours. Frustrated, he thought that perhaps praying the Stations of the Cross would make the time move by faster. He arose and went to the first station and began to pray. When he finished, he returned to his pew and noticed that the other seminarians had left. There was a note on his prayer book that read, "We did not want to disturb your prayer, so we left. We will be back at four o'clock to pick you up." He looked down at his watch. It was 4:15.

The young men had arrived at the church at one o'clock. He does not know when the others left, but they returned around 4:15. The experience this young man had in praying the stations is one of the most significant experiences he has had. He has been a priest now for over twenty-five years, and he's fond of telling people how important it is to push through whatever feelings they may have and make time for the Lord. The Lord is always generous with the little time we offer him.

CHAPTER FOUR

Pray As You Are

And he gave some as apostles, others as prophets, others as evangelists, others as pastors and teachers to equip the holy ones for the work of ministry, building up the body of Christ. (EPHESIANS 4:11–12)

ST. JOHN PAUL II WAS fond of reminding the various groups of people to whom he spoke, "Be who you are!" Young people, married couples, consecrated men and women throughout the world heard this important reminder. I first heard him speak these words at World Youth Day in Denver in 1993. It was an exciting time, one of great hope and promise, and his words struck at the heart of what so many of us too easily forget. The Father calls each one of us to accept and live out the unique task he has entrusted to us. Our vocation therefore defines how we are to be in the world, forming and shaping every facet of our lives. St. John Paul II sought to instill a sense of confidence in our ability to be the person God has created and called us to be.

His friend St. Teresa of Calcutta knew this as well. Often when I was with her during her visits to the United States, someone would tell her they wanted to be just like her by going to Calcutta and caring for the poorest of the poor. Mother always had the same response, "Don't come. There is one Mother Teresa of Calcutta…me. You must do whatever Jesus wants you to do, wherever he asks you to do it, and do it with great love. I am doing what Jesus has asked me to do."

The inspiring lives of the saints can lead us to want to become just like them, but as Mother knew, their lives should instead encourage us to say yes to whatever the Lord asks of us. This is an extremely important lesson to learn right at the start. It is common that people eager to climb the heights of spiritual perfection often attempt to adopt a life of prayer they admire in someone else. Seminarians often fall into this temptation. In their eagerness to please the Lord, they frequently heap all sorts of burdens (pious and penitential practices) upon themselves, burdens Jesus never asks them to carry.

I once led a day of recollection at a seminary (probably the one and only time) and I told the men in formation the following: "If after ordination you are planning on living off boiled potatoes and a little red wine, spending all your free time in the confessional of your parish church, don't! We already have a St. John Vianney. What may have worked in eighteenth-century France probably will not work in the twenty-first century in the United States. Instead, why not become the saintly parish priest that Jesus wants you to become?" If we are spending our time trying to make ourselves into the person we imagine God wants us to be, we will, no doubt, fail to recognize the person he actually needs us to become.

It is an essential and important truth of the spiritual life that God knows us better than we know ourselves. We are not in charge of who we should become! No matter how spectacular the person we have in mind, God alone defines each one of us. From all eternity, God has known the persons he created us to be, and knows us better than anyone else, including parents, siblings, friends, and spouses. Our greatest responsibility is to allow his Spirit to form us according to the divine plan. The full abundant life Jesus promises will only come about to the extent that we become the person God desires us to be. We must always yield to God. This is what it means to die to self. Only this will allow his work to reach its completion. Whenever we try to take control and tell the Lord who we think we should become, we end up discouraged and disappointed, and we may eventually even come to resent God.

It does not bother me that I am not John Vianney, Claude de la Colombière, Padre Pio, Maximilian Kolbe, or Josemaría Escrivá. While I greatly admire the lives of these men and so many other women and men in our family of faith, I am not them, and they, thanks be to God, are not me. My singular hope is that the virtues that appeal to me in their lives might bear fruit within my own, as I become evermore the Fr. Gary Caster that God longs to have me be.

Personally, I find this wonderfully freeing. I admit that it used to be a bit frustrating and disappointing that I didn't seem to be growing into the incredible Fr. Gary I had envisioned. Now I laugh when I compare that to the man—the priest—God is helping me to become. The things God continues to teach me about myself, I never would have learned in the super-priest version of my own imagination. In our daily willingness to yield to the Father's plan, we find true freedom and lasting peace. I have learned that the plan of God is much more exciting than anything I ever could have fashioned for myself.

The impulse to become like the people we admire can become a great hindrance to our spiritual life. Our vocation, or state of life, should form our life of prayer and spiritual practices. "Pray as you are," is a simple way to remember this. I am not a hermit, a monastic, or even a mendicant friar. I am a secular priest. However attractive certain characteristics of those other vocations may be, God has not called me to those ways of life. While I may include aspects of their spiritual practices, they cannot be to the detriment of my vocation as a diocesan priest. In other words, I cannot shut myself in the rectory, avoiding parishioners and living a semi-hermetic life. Nor can I neglect the needs of the people I serve because the rule of life I have imposed upon myself takes precedence over serving them.

This is true for every member of the Church. Married women should not have the same regimen of prayer as consecrated virgins or religious sisters. Married men should not pray like diocesan priests, mendicant friars, hermits, or monks. People that have yet to learn the way in which the Lord wants them to serve him should structure their life of prayer with an openness to learning God's plan. The structure of my prayer life is determined by the promises I made on the day I was ordained. Alongside that which I have promised, I have incorporated practices that enable me to adhere to Christ without preventing me from serving him as I have been ordained to do.

I know of a spouse whose piety was more important than marriage and family life, someone that refused to follow this simple, fundamental principle. Because of spending nearly every moment of every day lying prostrate before the Blessed Sacrament, the marriage ended. The children, feeling unloved and unwanted gradually turned to self-destructive behaviors. One of them is now in prison for life.

So please, pray as you are and not as you wish or think you should. Always be faithful to your state of life, your vocation, for by it, God will sanctify you. In the seemingly mundane, ordinary circumstances of your life, the most extraordinary and unexpected thing can happen: You become a saint!

CHAPTER FIVE

When to Pray

Rejoice in the Lord always. I shall say it again: rejoice!
Your kindness should be known to all. The Lord is near.
Have no anxiety at all, but in everything, by prayer and
petition, with thanksgiving, make you requests known
to God. Then the peace of God that surpasses all understanding will guard your hearts and minds in Christ
Jesus. (PHILIPPIANS 4:4–7)

EVERY FACET OF JESUS'S LIFE reveals the mystery of the divine.
His words and gestures, his interactions with others—relaxing
with friends, eating in people's homes, traveling from place to
place, praying with the community in the synagogue—gives
praise and glory to the Father. Like Jesus, every facet of our
lives should do the same. Through the Spirit given us, changing
diapers, grocery shopping, sitting through boring meetings,
shopping at Walmart, polishing brass, pulling weeds, driving
to work, indeed, every human activity becomes a means of
praising God. As St. Paul encourages us, we can pray without
ceasing by the manner in which we live our lives. However, in

order to do so, we, like Jesus, must set aside substantive time each day to speak with and listen to the Lord.

So when is the right time to go off to a quiet place and pray? First, it is important to identify a period of time that will be the same each day. When we vary the time, we end up making Jesus an agenda item, one of the many things we have to fit into our schedules. Continuity and consistency are hallmarks of a mature spiritual life. The time we spend in communion with the Lord must never become something on our to do list but should be a priority that blends with the rhythm and pattern of our lives.

No one has a schedule that precludes the possibility of identifying the right time for prayer. It could very well mean creating such a time by getting up earlier or staying up later. It could mean changing nonessential habitual activities like watching a show, reading a book, talking on the phone, listening to the radio, or using the computer. Yet every one of us can make time to be with the Lord in a substantive way. Do you commute to work alone? What are you doing in the car, on the train or bus? How long is your commute? You just may have found a block of time!

Stay-at-home parents usually have the greatest difficulty identifying a block of time to spend in conversation with the Lord. For obvious reasons, infants and toddlers often resist patterns and schedules, so this can make finding the right time seem unrealistic. This is when spouses need to help each other. If you are married, your primary responsibility is to see that your spouse gets to heaven, so helping facilitate a time for her or for him to be alone in conversation with God is your sacred duty. Whether employed or at home, both are working each day for the good of the family. Helping one another identify or create the time for serious and substantive conversation with the Lord also works for the spiritual good of the family.

Our culture treats time as a valuable commodity, as something never to be wasted. Therefore, we cling to it as if it is precious, worried we will never have enough. We are therefore wary of any demands made on our time. Mother Teresa told me that as long as I made time for God, he would give me all the time I needed.

When I met her, I was in grad school, but I was also teaching, writing a dissertation, and working five days a week at a home for people dying with HIV/AIDS. I am embarrassed to say that on many occasions, the volunteer work seemed an extraneous demand on my time. Yet, in yielding to Mother's advice (though not always with great alacrity), I learned that she was right. I am still amazed at how much can be accomplished in a single day when God remains my priority. Time does in fact stand still or even stretch out. Think about Christmas Eve when you were a child. It was the longest night of the year. Time seemed to drag on and on, and morning refused to come.

We should not become slaves to time but live like God, unbound by time's constraints. This is important when you begin to be alone with the Lord in prayer. Being absolutely fixated on the amount of time that has been set aside, down to the last second, is a common tendency. "I set aside twenty minutes, so I'm going to sit here until the twenty minutes are up." Avoid this at all costs. It treats God as a cruel taskmaster, a clock-watcher, rather than the fount of love that has invited you into his presence. Eventually, you will come to resent having to sit there until time runs out.

One of the most beautiful things that happens once spending time daily with the Lord becomes a habit is that your time together will often expand beyond what has been set aside. You will also come to recognize when your time together is concluded, which may even come before the clock runs out. Going away to a quiet place to pray is not about making time for God; it is about acknowledging and being grateful for the fact that God always has time for you. You do not undertake this time to prove God's importance in your life, but rather because it is necessary for life itself.

So how much time should be set aside each day for the Lord? If you are just beginning, I would suggest ten minutes a day. Now, on the face of it, this amount should not seem too daunting. We all waste more than ten minutes a day. On the other hand, ten minutes may seem like an insignificant amount. It is important to remember that the quality matters more than the quantity. Besides, you are building a habit that will extend throughout your life, so keep it simple. Your relationship with God will grow and expand like any other necessary and cherished relationship. You will soon discover that the ten minutes will become fifteen, and the fifteen, twenty, and so on.

———— ❦ ————

CHAPTER SIX

Where to Pray

When you pray, go to your inner room, close the door, and pray to your Father in secret. And your Father who sees in secret will repay you. (MATTHEW 6:6)

THE OBVIOUS ANSWER TO THE question is, anywhere and everywhere, "walking in public or strolling alone…seated in your shop…while buying or selling…or even while cooking" (St. John Chrysostom). There are no limits.

When I was teaching high school, I used to work out at a local fitness center that many of the students used. They would see me running on the treadmill at night, praying my rosary. Often students asked me, "Does praying on the treadmill count?"

I think there is a special place in purgatory for the person that originated the notion that some places count more than others do. Did this individual ever consider what this implies about the God who longs for us? Imagine God saying, "I'm not listening, Gary, because you are on the treadmill." That is certainly not the God of Jesus Christ. The Father always hears us, whenever and wherever we cry out to him.

Just to be clear, one of my favorite places in the world to pray is the Blessed Sacrament Chapel in St. Peter's Basilica in Rome (I prefer sitting in the left-hand corner if you're facing the tabernacle). The trouble is, I do not live in Rome, and I am rarely there. When Jesus tells his followers to go their rooms to pray, he is speaking about our capacity for interiority. He is not referencing a specific location. While designated places of prayer are invaluable, not everyone has regular access to them. What each of us can do, however, is fashion a prayer space of our own. Many martyrs of the Church turned their prison cells into great oratories where they poured out their souls to Christ. Many horrific, inhuman spaces have been consecrated by the women and men that used them as a place to commune with God. I think of Maximilian Kolbe singing God's praises in solitary confinement while dying. I also think about all the lives saved because faithful members of Christ's body prayed outside or across the street from abortion clinics.

It would be great if every day when we go off by ourselves to pray we could do that in a chapel where the Blessed Sacrament is reserved. This is unrealistic, and not even what the Church commands. For this reason, when we do have occasion to be alone with God in the presence of his Eucharistic Son, we should be grateful. Nevertheless, most of us will spend the majority of our alone time in our homes (or perhaps for commuters, in our cars, on public transportation, or walking). It is important that the space we use, like the time we spend, be the same. Our familiarity with designating a particular space for prayer will help move us into meditative, reflective conversation.

I have set aside a corner of my bedroom. I use the chair I sit in to pray only for that purpose. I place nothing on it, nor do I sit in it to tie my shoes or talk on the phone. I use it only for prayer, and the little stand that is next to it holds only my prayer book (and a statue of the Little Flower and a picture of Mother Teresa and a chaplet to the Blood of Christ). When I enter into this precious little space, I know I am doing so to be in the presence of God.

The choice of location is extremely important. Ideally, the chosen place should not be the center of commotion and activity. A quiet place that is comfortable, soothing, and familiar lends itself to what we are about, namely a retreat into the interiority of our hearts. We should be physically comfortable and as free from all external distractions as possible. A cramped awkward space next to noisy appliances, loud neighbors, and other intrusive noise is not necessarily helpful, especially when starting out. If you chose to make a prayer space outside, on a stoop, a patio, or a balcony, keep in mind the same parameters.

Should you choose a space favorited by your dog or cat, they need to learn you are not there to give them attention. They will learn over time and will even pray themselves. I had a cat that would join me each morning in the chapel in the house I lived in at the time. She would come in and sit calmly next to me the entire time I was at prayer. I know she was blessing the Lord just as dolphins and all water creatures do. My iguanas, snake, and parrots, on the other hand, never blessed the Lord in the chapel. Where I live now, a beaver that lives on the river where I fly-fish likes to sit next to me while I say Morning Prayer. As the sun crests over the mountains, we sit side by side (about fifteen yards apart) and together bless the Lord. That beaver is extremely devout.

Wherever I have lived, I have created a place that I use only for conversation with the Lord. I have found this to lend itself well to the task. I know this may appear to be difficult for those with young children at home, so a little creativity may be helpful. Tell your children what you are doing and why. This can be a great teaching tool. For those that are married, work together on identifying the right space.

If in identifying a regular time you decide that the commute to work offers the best opportunity, then make certain your car is properly equipped (e.g., a clean interior). What also may be helpful is a holy card affixed to the dash, a rosary hanging from the rearview mirror (if legal), and a bottle of holy water that can be used to bless the interior before you begin your drive. The Missionaries of Charity always pray when driving from point A to point B, even if only driving a block. I rarely have passengers in my car and am not in the habit of listening to the radio, so I constantly talk to the Lord while driving. You will be surprised at how quickly you will look forward to and become accustomed to the drive because it means you are alone with the Lord.

In truth, we can consecrate any space to the Lord, but we should give special attention to ensure that our prayer is not competing with whatever else may regularly be going on in the space (for instance, the bathroom). For many, the bathroom may be the only place to grab a quick few moments alone, which is fine, but it should not become the go-to place for substantive time with the Lord. This is not to suggest that the demands of the body are bad (the Jewish people have a prayer that is said after having attended to the needs of the body); it is simply that everything about the space can be an obvious hurdle to overcome. I pray in my bathroom every morning. While I shower, I renew my baptismal promises as the water falls over me. It proves to be a concrete way of reminding myself that I do reject Satan, his works and empty promises. I also affirm what I believe because of the person I have become.

Insofar as we all experience many natural distractions, it is important that the place we choose in being alone with God does not have too many built-in or customary distractions. Having said this, if you find that the only place in your home available to steal away and be with God is the bathroom (the tub, shower, etc.), then have at it. Be sure, however, to do something similar to what I mentioned about the car. Sprinkle some holy water and physically make the room a place for prayer. Do not simply do this in your mind. It must be a physical, overt act. I will explain how important this is when talking about what we should say.

————— ∞∞∞ —————

CHAPTER SEVEN

What to Say

When you pray say: Father, hallowed is your name, your kingdom come. Give us each day our daily bread and forgive us our sins for we ourselves forgive everyone in debt to us, and do not subject us to the final test. (LUKE 11:2–4)

NOW THAT YOU HAVE IDENTIFIED a place suitable for spending time alone to speak with the Lord heart to heart, the obvious question is, "What do I say?" Just as it is important to frame each day, we must also frame the time we set aside for this essential interior conversation. It is not a matter of merely bursting forth with anything on your mind and in your heart. What is necessary before such outbursts is reaffirming the liturgical nature of this time. I simply mean to emphasize that designating this way of being with the Lord is as important as the care you took in designating the place and the time. That is what liturgy does for us: It reminds us through words and gestures (and with what we wear), that the activity we engage in is not the same as other social activities like attending a concert, an assembly, a sporting event. Liturgy reminds us that not everything we do is of equal significance or value. Gathering with the community to praise God is certainly not the same as gathering with others for a sporting event. While each have a place in our lives as human beings, they are not equal. Praising God is of greater significance than cheering for our favorite team.

It is true that each of us is equal in dignity before God and the law, but that is where equality ends. We are not all the same or capable of achieving the same outcomes. I am not like everyone else; I am unique. God has created me specially such that no one can replace me, including another priest. I am the one and only Father Gary (thanks be to God!). This holds true for the time I set aside for God both alone and with the community of Christ's body. That time transcends everything else I do, and that is why it is essential that my life is built around such times.

Therefore, in order to solemnize my prayer time, I should begin the way we Catholics begin all our communal prayer. Namely, by slowly and reverently making the Sign of the Cross. Of itself, this is one of our greatest prayers. When concluded, we should acknowledge that we have come into the presence of the Lord. After making the Sign of the Cross, I say, "Lord, I believe that you are really present to me, that you see me, you hear me, you love me, and have called me into your presence. Thank you for letting me have this time alone with you." Whatever words you use to underscore that this time is like no other, I suggest it become your regular entrance antiphon. It has become so much a part of my lexicon that whenever I enter the eucharistic presence of the Lord, I automatically say the same thing. The words naturally draw me toward the Lord because they remind me of the truth that God is present to me and always listening.

Once I have begun my personal liturgy, I take a few moments just to be still and quiet. I savor being with the Lord. This does not mean I necessarily feel anything. It simply affords me the chance of not taking control. Remember, this time you share with the Lord is not and should never be thought of as a means to an end. It is an end in and of itself. That is why I do not rush into a colloquy of needs or worries or frustrations. I just sit with God, held in his grasp, and feel content. I know the one that has called me to himself and I know that he embraces me. Even if I never say a word, I will gladly make time each day to allow the Lord to hold me in his arms. After the first letter I received from Mother Teresa, she sent me a picture of an infant nestled in the palm of a hand. Off to the side, she wrote two words, Gary and God. From the word "Gary," she drew a line to the figure of the child; from the word "God," she drew a line to the hand. That was the extent of her note. No other words, just her signature. Every morning when I go off to pray, I become the drawing that she sent me.

Resting in the palm of God's hand may seem awkward at first. Thus I recommend to people that are just beginning to frame their time by reading the words of a psalm (it does not have to be the whole psalm either). There are numerous compact editions of the psalms, but I find the Catholic publication *Magnificat* to be a wonderful resource. Among the great treasury of prayers and reflections it contains, it has an abbreviated morning and evening prayer. When you go to your quiet place, make the Sign of the Cross, thank the Lord for calling you into his presence, sit quietly for a moment, and then simply read the lines of a psalm. When you have finished, sit peacefully with the Lord. The conversation should be natural and unforced. The words of the psalm might linger in your thoughts, which is a good thing. The psalms provide us the perfect vocabulary for talking with the Lord and sharing what is in our hearts. Maybe one of the words or expressions of the psalmist will resonate with you. Once again, it is important to remember that your only purpose is to become comfortable and familiar with speaking sincerely with the Lord. The words of the psalm are extremely helpful when you are not sure what to say. You can always repeat them, filling your time with them. Before I begin my quiet reflective time with the Lord, I pray Morning Prayer (which I promised the Church I would do). The words are the perfect background music for our time together.

If you find yourself thinking about the psalm used to begin your time of prayer, ask questions about it. "What brought about these words or feelings? Have I ever felt this way? If I had to sing a song before the Lord, what would my song be?" The psalms offer such an opportunity of deep reflection and meditation that if the words are touching your heart, do not push them away.

As you start to become more relaxed being with the Lord this way, try not to become too concerned with what you think you should be saying. The words will come as your comfort increases. If you have never done this before, spend the first few weeks taking in the awkwardness, the discomfort, the nagging doubt about whether or not and to what extent this is accomplishing anything. All such feelings are normal. You can even tell the Lord things like, "I don't even know if this is working.

This is silly. Are you even there? How will I know when you are speaking to me? OK, I am doing this but I don't think that priest knows what he's talking about."

We live in an outcome-based culture, so wondering about the efficaciousness is to be expected. St. John Vianney had a parishioner that would come from the fields into the church at the end of the day and sit before the tabernacle.

When the saint asked the man what he and Jesus talked about, the man simply said, "I look at him and he looks at me."

That was enough. The response was so moving to St. John, it brought tears to his eyes.

The Little Flower, St. Thérèse, said she liked to sit and simply gaze at the face of God because you learn everything by looking at a person's face.

The sure sign of the efficaciousness of the time you spend alone with the Lord is your desire to continue doing so. The Spirit of the Lord acts on us without force or violence. The subtly of God can be frustrating for those of us that want to be transformed in an instant. Yet faith assures us that God is at work in those who believe. As long as we make time for God, then his work within us will continue unto the day of Christ Jesus. My students often become restless with wanting signs of progress. At such times, I ask them three questions, "Did you pray yesterday? Did you pray today? Do you want to pray tomorrow?" If the answer to these three questions is yes, then I tell them everything is fine. Be patient, be trusting, and be at peace. Often they want to do more, but the many devotional and pious things we can do are meaningless activities if they do not flow from a heart that is rooted in the Lord. Through the composure of the heart, the Lord will draw us ever closer to himself.

The next obvious question is "How do I know when the Lord is speaking?" Jesus told us that his sheep know his voice, so rest assured you can and will know when he is speaking to you. However, in order to do so, you must be listening correctly. Too often, we try to listen as narrowly as possible, restricting our attention to preconceived notions of appropriate attentiveness. What we should be doing is listening as broadly as possible, being attentive and open to however the Lord choses to make his word known. Do not try to ignore the sounds that waft intermittently about you (like grumbling stomachs, the tick of a clock, a plane flying overhead, or other noises). Linger with them. In fact, hum along with the humming noises, measure the rhythm of the clanking, and mimic the grumbling. Let your mind move with them. Do not fight with them or with other sudden unexpected sounds. Only when we listen as widely as possible will the Lord's words fill our consciousness.

When it comes to prayer, we tend to treat everything as a distraction because we have created in our minds the way in which we expect the Lord to speak. The prophet Elijah made the same mistake. God did not reveal his presence in the way Elijah imagined. Instead, God showed himself in an imperceptible breeze (1 Kings 19:11–13). So listen widely, broadly, unafraid of the sounds around you. Once you stop fighting them, you will hear the Word of God. There is no mistaking it.

Of course, it does not always come as a sound, a word, or a statement. It can be a gentle nudge, an insight, a penetrating feeling. The Lord communicates to each one in a way proper to each. The way I understand him to be speaking to me may not be the way he speaks to you. God spoke to St. Joseph in dreams. The Lord knows how to touch our minds and hearts, for he has created us for himself. Familiarity with the Scriptures helps us to recognize the ways in which the Lord comes to us. I will talk more about them later.

Most often, the Lord moves within our hearts, conforming them to the Sacred Heart of his Son and building a beautiful reciprocity between the giving of ourselves and the giving of himself. Jesus said we will always know what to say concerning him, and that comes from our hearts resting in his. The infusion of knowledge happens so gradually, so subtly, that we are almost completely unaware. We only know that we must spend time with him, that we must listen attentively to the Scriptures, and that we must participate in the life of the community he has formed into his body. We must, because we know that if we do not, we will die. When my students ask me why I make so much time for prayer, I tell them it is because without it, I would not get out of bed in the morning. Prayer alone gives me life.

Just as there is a proper way to begin our time with the Lord, there is a proper way to end our time with him. St. Teresa of Ávila recommends that we conclude this time by thanking God for the chance of being with him and then praying aloud the Our Father. She knew how important it is that we hear ourselves pray.

Like Jesus, who often raised his voice to the Father, so must we. Vocal prayer is essential to living out our relationship with the Lord. We are not souls trapped in a body. We are embodied souls, so we must use our bodies to pray. People may tease

Catholics about standing, sitting, kneeling, even lying prostrate, but we pray with the whole of ourselves. A reverent bow, a deliberate and solemn Sign of the Cross, or a silent genuflection can convey more than a multitude of human words.

Listening to ourselves has a similar impact. It not only concretizes what we have undertaken, but it also embeds within our consciousness the fact that we have not been speaking to ourselves, that prayer is not a retreat into oneself but a movement toward God. I find that listening to myself pray is terribly humbling. Imagine me, an insignificant creature being able to speak to the Creator and author of all that exists, knowing that he wants to hear my voice. That is just so overwhelming to me, and especially humbling when I celebrate Mass. Listening to my words of prayer makes the experience remarkably tangible.

CHAPTER EIGHT

Sacred Scripture

> Know this first of all, that there is no prophecy of Scripture that is a matter of personal interpretation, for no prophecy ever came through human will; but rather human beings moved by the holy Spirit spoke under the influence of God. (2 PETER 1:20–21)

ALL CHRISTIANS SHOULD KNOW THE importance of sacred Scripture. After all, what is the Word of God, but the collection of writings that recount God's movement through history providing for us a way back to himself? As Catholics, we grow up traveling each Sunday through the pages of the Old and New Testament. If we are able to attend Mass during the week, we immerse ourselves in the Church's ongoing self-reflection in the passages set side by side with a psalm binding them together. At every important liturgical gathering and sacramental celebration, we hear God's Word proclaimed, affirming that what we are doing is not our own undertaking, but a work of God in which we are collaborators. The Scriptures are so essential to living fully our life of faith that we cannot know Christ without knowing them.

This does not mean, however, that we have to memorize everything preserved and handed down to us. I like to tell people, "I do not memorize Scripture; I live it." The Old and New Testaments are not just a precious, sacred reference guide; we should not treat them as a catechism or an encyclopedia. They are much more than a compendium of dogma. They are my memories and yours! I imagine most people do not think of them this way, but they should.

By the power of the Holy Spirit, the eternally begotten Son of the Father was incarnate in the womb of the Virgin Mary. In that moment, God assumed all of human history into the divine life. In the eternity of God, we have access to everything that has ever happened, from the first moment of creation up to the return of the Son of Man. Jesus's coming into the world encompasses far more than freeing us from eternal damnation. While his ministry has saved us from sin and death, it has also provided the means by which we can, here and now, live our humanity in all its rich possibilities. Created for the generous, limitless, unimaginable life of God, we, in Christ, have access to all that belongs to him. Jesus holds nothing back from us, including both his personal history and that of his people.

Thus, the stories contained in the Old Testament as well as in the Gospels are not anecdotes from the past. They are as much my memories as they are Abraham's, Ruth's, King David's, Luke's, John's, Mary's, and everyone else that is part of the story of God's love for us. Through, with, and in Christ, I am able to recall every sacred moment as my own because in Christ they are my own. Through the Spirit that Christ has poured into my heart, I can recall events from our sacred past as a participant, not an observer. The Scriptures are living because they live in me and I live in them. They tell the story of my life precisely because they tell the story of the life of the Son of God. Jesus promised his followers that we would be able to recall all things concerning him. I know this to be true because I take him at his word. Through the Spirit, he opens his life within mine. Jesus allows me to share all of salvation history, as I need to know it, and that means as my own. My life and your life are of biblical significance.

I am always fascinated how little we believe the incredible claims of our faith and their implications. For example, we believe that at baptism, the Trinity takes up a dwelling within us. Few actually live the implications of this truth. You, I, and everyone baptized into Christ takes God everywhere we go. We communicate the presence of God even if we do not mention him. Imagine intentionally living this truth of the faith. Imagine the lives that will be touched by our willingness to be what we have become. Imagine knowing that you bring God into your meetings, the supermarket, your athletic competitions, the classroom, etc. We are never alone, we have with us at all times all that we need, if only we believe.

I can tell you as a priest that most people—through no fault of their own—live as if God is far away, dwelling in some distant heaven. I always know where God is: wherever I am. Moreover, I always know at any given moment, exactly what God is thinking: He is thinking of me, of Gary. I suggest it is time for all the faithful to live intentionally the truths of our faith. All of salvation history exists within the life of the Trinity. The Trinity dwells within me; therefore, all of salvation history is my history.

I imagine that thinking of the Scriptures the way I have described them might take some getting used to, but what is the alternative? Treating them as if they are ancient, static memories of others. St. Ignatius of Loyola knew them as anything but static and unapproachable. He even came up with a way for his followers to take their place literally within them. I am certainly no saint, but I know exactly what Ignatius wanted his confreres to experience. Living this way did not win me many friends during my years of formation, but I can tell you it has changed the lives of many followers of Christ since then.

The conviction I have through faith and the power of the Holy Spirit (cf. 1 Thessalonians 1:5), enables me to say that I know much more about Jesus than what is contained in the four Gospels, just as I know much more about Jeremiah, Jacob, and Ruth, and all in my family of faith. Benedict XVI described believers as "custodians of memory," one of my favorite descriptions of belief. In Christ, we have become a people whose memories (intertwined within the Church's own) are a witness to and compendium of God's love. We share space with all that God has accomplished in time. Therefore we now are able to punctuate the historical time in which we live with everything God has done and all that he yet longs to do (cf. 1 Colossians 1:24–29).

These words remind me that I am always much more than what people see when they encounter me, or even what they think of me once they have. Christ lives in me! I am the repository of everything God hopes for humanity! I may seem insignificant, the least likely to be a Christian, let alone a priest, but my life nonetheless moves within the spirations of the Trinitarian persons. My life moves about in realms unimaginable, places "eye has not seen, ear has not heard," places wholly unthinkable. You and I are the only Gospel many people will ever encounter. Imagine the possibilities if each member of Christ's body awoke each morning excited to live this truth of our faith. The fact is, they can; and it is not such a difficult thing to do.

The only thing making it difficult is those nagging doubts that have as their source the Prince of Darkness. He has only one trick (and Satan hates it when I give away his one trick), and that is to make us doubt God's love for us. Satan cannot read our minds or force our behavior. Satan's great intelligence enables him to make assumptions about our inherent weaknesses concerning God. Yet he cannot force us to act on them. All Satan can do is instill doubt. I have always told my students that if Satan is bothering them, they should tell him, "Go bother Father Caster. Leave me alone."

I am glad they do. Once, while my sister was dying, lightning struck the house in which we were staying. After the emergency responders had left, my sister said to me, "Would you stop telling your students to send Satan to bother you?" Of course, she said this with great love and only a little bit of frustration. She knew that I went to any lengths to protect them. She also knew that I really enjoy telling Satan to go to hell.

On my way to the airport the next day, the student that had sent the principalities of darkness my way phoned to apologize, not knowing about the lightning.

I told the young man, "You did the right thing, and boy Satan was not happy about it."

I explained the events of the previous night, and we laughed about the predictability of the evil one. When the young man was married, I told the story during my homily.

Why is it that I would propose such a thing as to invite others to send the powers of darkness my way? It is all due to what I have been trying to explain about the place of Sacred Scripture. I was not historically in the desert with Jesus, but because I share his life, I am with him in the desert and in every other moment of his life. Being with Jesus in the desert, I learned how to talk to and treat the great deceiver. Standing with Jesus in the desert enables me to stand against Satan now. I also know what it is like to have Jesus hold me. I am the pillar against which they scourged him. Reading the Scriptures should not be an activity of the spiritual life, but a necessity for daily life.

You may be thinking—and rightly so—"How do I find time to speak sincerely with the Lord and read the Scriptures? I thought you said this was the spiritual life made *simple*." Driving these questions and initial criticisms is our contemporary preoccupation with a general lack of time. We must be familiar with Sacred Scriptures, but that familiarity comes about naturally. I am not suggesting that you set out to read the Bible from the first to the last page. The beauty of our Catholic faith is that the Church presents the Scriptures to us on a daily and weekly basis. The primacy of the spiritual life will always be the time spent alone in conversation with the Lord, but that will only flourish to the extent that we are engaged with an ongoing education in coming to know the Lord. The Scriptures facilitate this education.

If you are able to attend Mass only on Sundays, do you read

the Scriptures ahead of time, including the night before? I refuse to believe this is impossible. We make time for everything we deem important, including much that, in the face of eternity, is wholly insignificant. I am not suggesting an intellectual excursus on the passages for any given weekday or Sunday; I am talking about having in your mind the words the Church proclaims. You can even follow along with them.

I receive an email each day from the USCCB (United States Conference of Catholic Bishops) with the daily Scripture readings, including those for Sunday. I can tell you it usually takes me between one and a half and two minutes to read the Scriptures. I personally like to do this after my alone time with the Lord, but you may want to begin your prayer time by reading them (or a psalm, as I mentioned above). Again, you should not be concerned with memorizing, but with familiarizing. If you do this every day, in a year's time, you open yourself to a huge portion of the Bible, and you do so within the life of the Church. That is, as the Church celebrates the saving work of Christ. This is the best context for reading and learning the Scriptures.

This will have a dramatic impact on the time you spend with God. The two will naturally spill into each other, the Scriptures informing your conversation and your conversation opening you to things in the Scriptures you never before considered. You will come to know Jesus more intimately, the one that gave his life up for you, and the Father who has been working ceaselessly to have you once again in his loving embrace. You will also become much more familiar with the Holy Spirit, for the Spirit makes all of this possible. God does not want to be probed, dissected, and taken apart as some high school experiment or examined like some graduate-school thought exercise. God wants us to know him from within, and Jesus is the way into the life of God. The Scriptures accompany us along the way into the hidden riches of divine life.

During one of Mother Teresa's visits to Washington, DC, I accompanied her to the convent of her contemplative sisters. The tour of the convent ended in the fenced-in backyard where the sisters were preparing to start a garden. In the corner of the yard, there was a large mound of dirt and fertilizer. One of the sisters that had traveled with Mother from India climbed to the top of the mound and, putting her hands in the air, turned completely around.

Smiling she looked down at me and said, "Baby priest, you can see all the world from here, even the mountain where Jesus taught us the Beatitudes. Come see."

After she came down, I cautiously climbed up the mound, and she was right. I could see the entire world. I could even see Jesus sitting on the side of the hill with people all around him, and I could hear him speaking.

Immediately I came down, a little unnerved by the experience, and sister said to me, "Baby priest, you just climbed into the Gospel. You never know what door will take you there."

Mother simply smiled.

This was the first of many lessons of our faith that Mother and her Missionaries of Charity would teach me.

CHAPTER NINE

The Sacraments

His divine power has bestowed on us everything that makes for life and devotion, through the knowledge of him who called us by his own glory and power. Through these, he has bestowed on us the precious and very great promises, so through them you may come to share in the divine nature. (2 PETER 1:3-4)

PATTERNED AFTER UNAMBIGUOUS, SIGNIFICANT MOMENTS in the life of Christ and instituted by him, the sacraments are a great gift of the Church. They draw us into the life of God and open us to God's loving care. From birth until death, we experience this loving care in concrete ways, through signs and symbols that really communicate that which they symbolize. Our personal faith and conviction do not impart power into the symbols used by the Church; Christ does. The efficacious nature of the sacraments is wholly a work of God, which the Church safeguards and celebrates. With or without our willingness to believe, God continues to offer himself to us because of his love and care.

The Creator of heaven and earth made the world with a view to the life, death, resurrection, and ascension of his only Son.

We can say then, that when God created, he had the sacraments in mind. They are not inventions of the Church; they are realities that flow from the same one that said, "Let there be…" and it came to be. The Jesuit poet Gerard Manley Hopkins wrote, "The world is charged with the grandeur of God." This is most certainly true with respect to the sacraments. Through them, God spoils us with his affection and attention, lavishing his love upon us in the real, concrete conditions and circumstances of our lives. The sacraments are perhaps the easiest way of letting God love us. Most likely, this is not what you learned about them, but it is nonetheless true.

Therefore, what I would like to do now is say a little something about each one of the seven, hoping to situate them better within the context of our lives of faith.

The Sacrament of Baptism

Do you remember the first gift your parents gave you? Do you know where it is or what became of it? What about all the gifts you just had to have as a child, an adolescent, or a young adult. Where are they now? What is the best gift you have ever given someone, and what is the best gift you have ever received?

The point I am trying to make should be obvious. The giving and receiving of gifts is a funny thing. We desperately and intensely want something that usually, in a short amount of time, becomes insignificant and unimportant. Each year we struggle to find the perfect gift for those we love and care for, only to repeat the same search the following year. This necessarily means the perfection of the gifts chosen before fades with time. Maybe they were not as perfect as we initially imagined.

The gift of baptism is nothing like this. It is perfect; it is the most important gift we will ever receive (even more important than Holy Orders). Its value never decreases. For me, everything in the spiritual life centers on the sacrament of baptism. Period. It is the only way into the life of God and the only way to share the life of Christ.

You already know that I think it is underappreciated. Yet I would like to reassert what I have said before. At the moment of our baptism, we are incorporated into Christ's body, and the Trinity dwells not only within, but the Trinity remains. I think the remains part is that which most people forget. In the vast majority of cases, it is no one's fault; it is merely a problem. As a public representative of the Church, I think it is my responsibility to help people appreciate better, experience more fully, and celebrate more actively the truths of our faith. I consider it my responsibility to help others to live intentionally their baptismal dignity.

I have already mentioned how significant it is that God accompanies us wherever we go. I thought therefore that I would mention another significant fact of our baptism that people also forget: through the Holy Spirit, we share in the priestly, prophetic, and kingly life of Christ. The implications of this are mind-boggling. You and me and all the baptized live in the world as Jesus lived in the world—with a status that flows from his relationship with the Father. The Father has given Christ all glory, honor, and kingship, and Jesus in turn shares this with us.

By sharing in the priestly life of Christ, we become able to make offerings to God. Taken from among the people and made representatives before God (cf. Hebrews 5:1), priests make offerings to God on behalf of others. Now, in Christ, we too are able to make offerings on behalf of others, because we are able to sanctify every dimension of our lives. Every act we undertake, no matter how seemingly insignificant, we are able to offer to the Father through, with, and in Jesus, his Son. When we lift something up to the Father, offering it for ourselves or for others, we exercise the priestly ministry of Christ. We do not have to ask someone to do this for us; we can make such offerings ourselves.

For many years, I resisted flossing my teeth. I consider flossing to be the twenty-first-century equivalent of flagellation (beating oneself with a knotted cord). It is an awkward, difficult, and messy practice. Some years ago, I mentioned this at a parish mission, and after my talk, a man came up to me and said, "Father, you just said that we can make anything an offering to God as an expression of our love for him. Why don't you floss as an expression of your love for God?"

It was as if Jesus said to me, "Physician, heal thyself." Of course, this man (a dentist) was right. I had been looking at flossing from the wrong perspective. I have been flossing ever since!

Sharing in the priestly life of Christ also enables us to speak to the Father as one person speaks to another. We do this not as strangers, but as his children. We can talk to God anytime we want, sharing what lies deep within our hearts. There is no longer any obstacle to our ability to draw near to the Lord. I am the only thing that stands in the way of my being with God.

Our participation in Jesus's prophetic life underscores the implications of this. Prophecy does not mean that we are able to predict the future. It means something far greater. We are now able to know the plan and will of the Father. We actually have access to the mind of God! Insofar as God hides nothing from us, nothing remains obscure.

What is the plan of God but that we share fully in his life? Through baptism, the divine life intermingles with our human, spiritual, and bodily life. As I have stated before, the transformation effected by the Spirit takes place without force or violence as God shares with us mysteries hidden before the ages. The more open we are to the learning that comes from on high, the better able we are to help others come to knowledge of the truth. It is not to a select few that knowledge of God's plan is given. Rather, it is made known to all that share life with Christ. All the baptized are equipped to speak on behalf of the one "that has blessed us in Christ with every spiritual blessing in the heavens" (Ephesians 1:3).

Our participation in the kingly life of Christ enables us to express in concrete ways the wisdom of God's plan because we are able to serve as Jesus served and to love as Jesus loved. Jesus expressed his royal mission not through control and domination, but through his willingness to lay down his life in love. By emptying himself and taking the form of a slave, he revealed the true nobility of God (cf. Philippians 2:7). Jesus expresses his royal mission through his life lived for others because he lives on every word that comes from the mouth of God. Jesus knows the Father will grant whatever he asks and that the Father attends to his every need. Jesus concerns himself only with what each day brings, never grasping at equality with God. Jesus emptied himself into every situation and circumstance he faced, manifesting his noble character in the simple, confident trust he had in the Father. No one could lay hold of Jesus. His life was wholly his own because in all things he resolutely handed it over to the Father.

Reigning with Christ means living just as he did. We too must empty ourselves, handing all things trustingly to our Savior. Our royal mission is to work toward bringing about a kingdom of justice, love, and peace. By laying down our lives and taking up our cross, we extend into the world the kingdom of God, even as we daily pray for its coming. Through love and service, we build up the kingdom of heaven on earth. Through love and service, we will inherit the land, for meekness derives from the strength to resist controlling, manipulating, and subjugating others. Our royal mission is to be emissaries of Christ, who came not to condemn the world, but to save it through sacrificial love. Participating in the kingly life of Christ does not mean we rule over the world. It means love rules over our hearts, animates our actions, and endures all things unto the coming of the Son of Man in glory.

The Sacrament of Confirmation

I have journeyed throughout the United States leading parish missions. Throughout my travels, I have learned firsthand how poorly the sacrament of confirmation is being presented and how woefully taught. Many parishes use it as a way to try to keep adolescents in religious ed, while other places treat it as a reward earned through service hours, rote memorization, and retreat attendance.

Sadly, many of the people that graciously volunteer to instruct young people throughout their preparation cannot themselves explain what difference the sacrament has made in their lives. Once, I told a group of young people that if their parents, guardians, or teachers could not tell them the difference confirmation has made in their lives, or at least the difference Jesus makes in their lives, they did not have to return. I thought the DRE was going to throw me out the window of their parish classroom. (Yes, at any given moment, I can tell you the difference confirmation has made in my life, and I can happily tell you the difference Jesus makes every day).

Confirmation is not a rite of passage into adulthood. Confirmation equips the believer to stop hiding behind doors locked out of fear and insecurity and boldly step forward as a follower of Christ. The reception of the Holy Spirit at baptism incorporates us into the Body of Christ and constitutes us as members of the Church. The reception of the Holy Spirit at confirmation empowers us to live in the world as followers of Christ by bestowing on us the gifts needed to live that which we have become.

In my day, the predominant image was that of being a soldier for Christ, armed with everything needed to protect ourselves from the battles that lie ahead. Like the apostles on Pentecost, we would no longer be afraid to call ourselves disciples of Christ. Rather, we would be emboldened to bring the Gospel wherever we went, primarily by the example of our lives and with words when asked to explain why we live the way we do. I found the imagery bold and spectacular. At least it lends itself to an intentional way of living, much more so than being an "adult Catholic," whatever that means.

The seven gifts of the Spirit that we receive are perfectly suited for the task of living intentionally in the world. How many times have you struggled to find the right words? Did you call on the gift of counsel? How many times have you not wanted to pray whether alone or with the community? Did you call on the gift of piety?

I call on these gifts every day. Before a student comes to see me and even while one sits across from me, sharing what is in his heart or on her mind, I say repeatedly in my thoughts, *Counsel, counsel, counsel.* I know the words I need to speak will come. I trust the gift I have received. If you ever had the experience of someone sharing with you that your words were just what they needed to hear, well, that is because of the gift of counsel. So call upon it more frequently.

Before I celebrate Mass or hear confessions, I call upon the gift of piety. I know I am the last man that should stand in the person of Christ, but I also know that the gift of piety will help push aside my insecurities and doubts so I can be present to those tasks for which the Church has ordained me. I cannot live without the gifts of the Holy Spirit. Real, ordinary daily life can challenge our resolve, make us question our loyalty, and dampen our spirits. I know how to battle against these challenges: the gifts of the Holy Spirit.

How great is it that the Lord imparts to us the gift of understanding. Many think we receive this gift in order that we might comprehend the ways of God, but we receive this gift primarily so that we can understand ourselves. The Lord taught us that we must love others as we love ourselves, which is only possible to the extent that we have a deep understanding of both our strengths and our weaknesses. St. Thérèse of Lisieux said she loved her nothingness; that is what kept her clinging to Christ. If you examine the lives of the saints, you will recognize that they all have a tremendous understanding of self. In book ten of his *Confessions*, St. Augustine begs to understand himself, to know himself as God does.

While it is true that knowing God loves me gets me out of bed in the morning, it is only through the gifts of the Holy Spirit that I can live through each day. That is why the gift of fortitude is so important in the life of each believer. We need a strength we cannot manufacture for ourselves. We need the reassurance that only the Spirit gives. Fortitude acts subtly with my own sprit, and I see its effects when I bite my tongue, when I act with prudence, when I do not allow external conditions and circumstances to determine my behavior. Always the Spirit is with us, imparting whatever we need in whatever situations we encounter. All we have to do is ask. It truly is that simple. Call on the Spirit and use the gifts you have been given. A quick prayer you may find helpful is "Come Holy Spirit, come through Mary."

The Most Holy Eucharist

Many Catholics are not aware that it was only in the early twentieth century that they were encouraged to receive the Eucharist more regularly. Prior to Pope St. Pius X's inspiration, Catholics did not—as a rule—receive the Eucharist when they listened to Mass, on Sunday. The obligation was to attend Mass each week and receive Communion at least once a year and, if possible, during the Easter season. I am so grateful for the change and the opportunity to receive the Lord as often as possible.

The reason is simple: Without the reception of the Holy Eucharist, one cannot live fully a life with Christ. What better way, therefore, to let God love us, than to receive the gift of love that is the sacrifice of his Son? Jesus does not want us to be spectators of the memorial of our redemption, but active participants. Each Sunday we have an opportunity to join with members of his Body, raising our voices with Jesus and with each other, thanking God the Father for the life, death, resurrection, and ascension of his Son. The Catholic Church describes the Eucharist as the "source and summit" of our Christian life. Therefore, we should gladly gather each week in praise and thanksgiving.

Of course, we know this is not always the case. I have often had people, young, old, and in between, complain that Mass is boring. I always reply the same way: "Mass is not boring; you are."

I learned this from my mother. Whenever we would complain, she would tell us that Jesus did not come to entertain or amuse us. He came to love us, and Mass is where we most intimately experience his love. When we complained about the new priest whose English was difficult to understand, she told us to make up our own homilies. We did. After Mass on the way to breakfast, she would ask each of us to share our homily. Of course, this soon became a competitive undertaking, thereby influencing our engagement. With great fondness, I remember those conversations. They were great times with my mother and my siblings. (My father was not yet Catholic). Oh, and we never again complained. I think my older brother actually preferred attending Mass with our new foreign priest.

The point of this is simple. Mass is not supposed to be entertaining. The homily is not the focus of the Mass. Whether the priest is a good orator should not matter. It also should not matter if he speaks perfect English. We do not come to Mass for the priest. We come to Mass to be in communion with Jesus, or at least we should be. We will never experience a perfect liturgy until we are in heaven. Until then, we should try to make every effort to ensure the solemnity of our liturgies, but they will always be the work of weak, finite, limited human beings. That means there will necessarily be room for improvement and plenty of distractions.

The morning after I met Mother Teresa, I joined with her and her sisters for Mass in their little chapel. Mother took her place on the floor, right next to me. This made me terribly nervous. We had to share a Missionary of Charity songbook, which I held in my shaking hands. However, that was not the worst of it. At the Sign of Peace, I did what most young American Catholics did at that time, and turned to hug her. As I was wrapping my arms around her, a voice inside my head, probably my guardian angel, screamed, "Stop!"

I did not. I trapped Mother in my embrace, and she stood completely still, like a pillar of stone. I was mortified, and could not wait for Mass to end. I just wanted to die. Talk about a distraction!

At the conclusion of every Mass, the sisters make a thanksgiving. When we had finished, Mother turned to me and said, "Come."

With great fear and trembling, I stood up and followed her.

She led me to the sacristy and said to the priest while he removed his vestments, "Monsignor, I must make confession. Gary has distracted me during Holy Mass." She then turned to me and smiled.

Mother Teresa had a tremendous sense of humor! No, she did not go to confession, but I sure wanted to go.

People often complained to Mother that they were distracted during Mass. She would put them at ease by reminding them about the many things that could be distracting. One's family or spouse, the servers, the readers, the priest, the music, and so on. The Church asks that we prepare to receive our Lord during Mass as best we can. I tell my students that when they find themselves distracted, just look up at the crucifix. Then simply tell the Lord, "I know you are the reason I am here. Thank you." If you find yourself distracted during Mass, or falling asleep, there is no need to feel as if you have let the Lord down. Simply collect yourself as best you can and find something upon which to focus your attention. Remember, his apostles could not even remain awake with him in prayer. He did not reject or abandon them. He will not reject or abandon you.

Our culture has negatively influenced the way in which we think about our communal gathering. Because there is music and stories (the readings) and a speech (the homily), we are conditioned to think that some kind of performance is taking place. However, nothing could be further from the truth. The words we hear proclaimed should call to mind the truth of who we are as they recount that which God has been doing throughout all of history. This should help us better prepare for the one that gives himself—sacramentally—to us.

Everything about Mass has Jesus and his sacrificial death as its focus, and also our communion with him. Through the action of the Holy Spirit, the mystery of our faith becomes present to us under the appearance of bread and wine. Through these elements, we "taste and see the goodness of the Lord" (Psalm 34:9), for we feast on the true food of his flesh and the true drink of his blood (cf. John 6:55). The whole movement of the liturgy leads us to the moment we will literally commune with Jesus. This is unimaginably spectacular.

Yet how is it possible that a flat, tasteless wafer and a tiny sip of mediocre wine (well, it certainly is not Veuve Clicquot or Châteuaneuf-du-Pape), communicate the life of the Son of God? The answer to this is quite simple. Jesus told us. If he is God, then he cannot lie.

I know that perhaps this is not a satisfactory answer for many, so I will propose another. If it is true that Jesus's death on the cross is the perfect expression of God's love for fallen humanity and that Jesus's sacrifice has reconciled us to the Father, then I must have true access to it. How can I say that I know the depth of God's love for me if the expression of that love remains a historical event? I cannot. I can know of God's unfathomable love only if I can personally, truly experience the immolation of his Son.

Each time we attend Mass, we do. In an unbloody way, the veil of time is torn, and we stand, as it were, on that hill outside Jerusalem. By the power of the Holy Spirit, we are drawn into the memorial of love with which he loved us to the end, and not symbolically. If the bread and wine we receive were incapable of communicating Jesus's love, then the entire Mass would be an empty gesture and a waste of time. It is only the fact of the bread and wine being transformed that enables me to experience truly the love of God. St. Thomas Aquinas says that it is only through faith that we understand the gift of the Eucharist, but for me personally, taken from the perspective of love, the Church's position makes perfect sense. Besides, if a virgin can have a baby, then anything is possible with God. I therefore have no doubt that in the Eucharist, I receive exactly what Christ offered humanity: his body and his blood.

This food sustains us as we follow him. This food nourishes our spirits, brings peace and joy to our souls. We may not be worthy to receive, but he extends himself anyway. Jesus came that we might have life, and through the Eucharist, we know that he means it because he truly gives us his life. Nothing should prevent us from being with the company of believers that gather each week to take part in this sacred activity.

The second best day of my mother's life was the day my father became Catholic, March 4, 1979. I was seventeen years old. He had been taking instruction without my mother's knowledge. He did not tell her because he did not want to hurt her should he decide not to follow through with it. From that moment on, my father came each week and led us to the front. He wanted to avoid the distractions of others and be "as close to the action as possible." He always received Communion on the tongue and would tear up as he received our Lord. I was the last person to offer Communion to my father, and once again, there were those beautiful tears. What a gift my father gave to me, what an example.

He never knew what his tears meant to me, just as we rarely know the gift we can be for another. I led a parish mission some years ago in central California and talked about how important it is for the rest of the community that we are present at Mass. How we may never even know the effect our presence may have on those that have gathered with us.

A man in his early twenties once shared this story to underscore my point. As he grew into his teens, he hated coming to

Mass and only came because his parents made him. This went on even as he entered college. However, since he lived at home, he had to go.

He told us that each week he would watch an elderly man, hunched and using a walker, make his way to Communion. One day the example of the elderly man shook him. He said to us, "Here I was sitting through Mass, mad at my parents for making me go, and there was that man, using all his strength to walk up and receive Communion. I was ashamed of myself. That was the moment of my conversion. That man, whom I never met and whose name I do not know, changed my life."

We never know the effect our presence can have on another. The ways of God are so far beyond our ways. We need each other; we need to be with the community gathered in prayer.

At one of the Newman Centers where I served as director, a young man came to see me because he knew Catholic priests could not repeat what they heard. He told me he was Catholic but that he no longer practiced the faith. He had come to college with his high school sweetheart and other mutual friends, but they had broken up, and he felt alone. He was uncomfortable being around the mutual friends and did not know what he should do.

I told him he needed a new community of friends. I suggested he come to some of our activities because there were many terrific people and he should get to know them. I said, "I do not care if you come to Mass or not. Just come meet the students here and see if this might not be the place for you to find new friends."

He began coming to our social events, then Mass, then made a retreat (which he later led), and joined us on pilgrimage. This young man not only found a company of friends and a community, but he met his wife, rediscovered his faith, and became one of our most prominent and delightful members.

THE SACRAMENT OF PENANCE

Mother Teresa had a tremendous, intelligent, satirical sense of humor. That is what I loved most about her. When she joked with me about needing to go to confession because I distracted her during Mass, she was not joking about the importance of the sacrament. While the heart of the life of every Missionary of Charity is the Eucharist, the way they "prepare for the meal that sustains their work" is the sacrament of penance.

Mother taught them that the confession of a child in sin always begets humility and that humility is strength. She understood confession as nothing but humility in action. We call it penance, but really, it is a sacrament of love. This sacrament of forgiveness is the place where we allow Jesus to take from us everything that divides and destroys. When our love is divided, whenever there is a gap between Christ and ourselves, anything can come and fill that gap. Confession prevents that from happening. It is a beautiful act of great love because by it, we tell the Lord and we show him that we do not want anything to come between him and ourselves.

Of course, we know this, right? We do not need Mother Teresa—however saintly and celebrated—to remind us of basic sacramental theology. When we sin, we must be reconciled to God. If we offend someone, we must say we are sorry. This is, after all, what we teach children. We do not tell them to do this in their hearts; we tell them this has to be out loud and to the person they offended.

Despite what we know and what we teach the young, I think we benefit from Mother's words. I say this because as we grow, we have an innate tendency toward abstractions. Without someone grounding us in reality (here I have in mind Our Lady), our natural movement with respect to faith is toward the abstract, the ethereal, toward "lofty ideas and noble sentiments" (to quote Benedict XVI). Much of the talk about the New Evangelization offers a good example of this. If I hear one more person talk about it as a better way to disseminate information or describe it as a program that really puts forward the rich, intellectual heritage of the Church, I will no doubt end up like Lot's wife.

What I believe we need is the method of Christ. In my mind, this is precisely what St. John Paul II and so many others understood the New Evangelization to be. Jesus's primary means of evangelization was through encounter. By meeting him, by watching him, people were open to listening to what he had to say. After all, nobody with authority had ever spoken this way (see Mark 1:22). Typically, encounter comes before any singular datum of faith. Jesus even sent the apostles out two by two into the towns he planned to visit. The encounter with the disciples prepared for the encounter with Jesus. Jesus never instituted a program; he sent people. Therefore, *we* must be the means by which others will encounter Christ. Nothing is more attractive than a heart aflame with Christ.

In other words, we are the Gospel ("the light of the world" and "salt of the earth"). We must be the means by which another person encounters Christ. This is especially true for me because I am a priest. If people are not meeting Jesus when they meet me, then I am just a functionary, a sacramental vending machine, a

Catholic Carnac the Magnificent who doles out theologisms for every envelope collected. I cannot imagine a worse way to live.

I think St. Teresa of Calcutta's words concerning the sacrament can help ground us so we do not to drift aloft in splendid cerebral isolation. She encourages us to experience the love of God through personal and concrete contact with his mercy. Thus, if we want to remain grounded in a lived, visceral experience of God lavishing his love upon us, we must have regular recourse to the sacrament of penance. It is a fact that we will never credibly encourage others to experience God's love this way, if it is not an existing fact of our relationship with the Lord. People will see right through us if we talk about the necessity of this sacrament for our spiritual lives but don't receive it regularly.

I understand how difficult talking about confession can be; I currently serve one of the most reluctant target audiences. Yet talk about it I do, with all its grandeur and all its clunky humanness. My students do respond, repeatedly. Since I share with them how I regularly avail myself of the sacrament, I have no doubt they think, *I wonder what Father's problems are that he has to go so frequently?* I am glad they wonder! I too am limited, weak, and vulnerable. I do not care that they wonder what my sins might be. I care that they know how much I need to root myself in God's mercy. The sacrament of penance is the best way for me to do so.

Perhaps this is what makes it difficult for all of us. We have to expose ourselves to another, to a man, to someone we know has his own quirks and limitations. Who in his or her right mind would want that someone should know that I do not have it all together, figured out, or locked in? Talk about humility!

Well, to push aside this understandable way of thinking, here are the words of our saint, "Confession is Jesus and I and nobody else. Remember this for life!" Whatever any priest might think of me after hearing my confession should not matter to me. It is all and only about Jesus and me. No one else. Whenever I wait to have my confession heard, I repeat Mother Teresa's words to myself, over and over again. "It is just me and Jesus, me and Jesus, me and Jesus." They calm my nerves and redirect my attention on exactly what matters: the mercy of God.

Not long after I was ordained, I spent New Year's Eve with Mother and her sisters at her convent in Rome. It was her idea; she wanted to celebrate my priestly ordination since she could not come to the United States for it. During the holy hour from eleven to midnight, Mother asked the priest I was with and me to hear confessions. Just before the holy hour began, Mother said to the two of us priests, "You are the towel Jesus uses to wipe clean the feet of his people. You must keep this towel clean for Jesus. You do this by your own willingness to make your souls clean by going to confession." Right away, I looked at the priest I was with and asked him if he would hear my confession. I wanted to be a suitable instrument for Jesus to wipe clean the feet of the sisters.

Our personal, individual recourse to the sacrament is not only a means to prevent our teaching about it from becoming abstract and disembodied. I learned from my years with Mother and the sisters that confession is perhaps the single greatest means by which I invigorate the daily work of my own ministry. It brings back to me that first encounter with Jesus, which took place when I was nine years old on a Thursday in June. Through the sacrament of penance, I am able—through God's grace and mercy, to reencounter him as I did in that initial moment that changed my life forever, that moment when he touched my shoulder and said, "I love you Gary. I have always loved you. I will always love you. You will always matter to me. I will never leave you. There is something I want you to do for me that only you can do."

Anyone that knows me will tell you this encounter with Christ did not all at once perfect me in charity or all the other Christian virtues. Rather it convicted me of Christ's love and made me believe that charity and all the other virtues could be mine—in him. It made me believe with St. Thomas Aquinas that I could actually want—intend—all that Christ wants and intends for me. When I am a penitent, I do not think of heaven or hell, state of grace or any of the finer points of theology. I think only that Jesus is once again making himself present to me, saying in words so often used by Mother speaking in the voice of Christ, "You are precious to me. I love you. You have called me by name; you are mine; you are why I died on the cross."

In the intimacy of the moment, I know how necessary the sacrament is and that there is no greater power in restraining the disordered passions of my soul and in subjugating my appetites to right reason. It all comes together in an instant, despite the confessor, and let me tell you, I have had more than my share of men that should never have been given the permission to hold another human being's soul in their hands.

As Mother so often told her daughters, this encounter with Christ is only possible through humility. Knowledge of oneself is necessary for the reception of God's mercy. Mother said this is the reason the saints could say they were "very wicked criminals." They saw God, and they saw themselves, and they saw the difference. She was convinced that when the saints looked upon themselves with such horror, they really meant it. They were not pretending.

I know for a fact she looked upon herself this way. Many times, I heard her tell people that when we come into the world, we come in with our hands closed in a fist. Throughout the whole of our lives, God tries to pry open our fingers so that our hands are empty before him, and thus we can do the work of "feeding his flock." She would end by holding up her hands all the fingers raised except one pinky and say, "I am still fighting God over this little finger."

We should go to the Lord empty-handed, holding nothing, clinging to nothing, grasping nothing. In the sacrament of penance, the Lord works to pry our fingers free so that we can receive from him everything he longs to give to us and to those we serve. For Mother, the sacrament of penance is so much more than simply caring about one's own salvation, about getting into heaven. It is all about serving the Lord, quenching his hunger and thirst by tending the unwanted, the unloved, and the uncared for, the hungry, the naked, the homeless, the lepers, the alcoholics.

Of course, in order to do this, to be able to work, to be able to see, to be able to love, we need the Eucharist, the intimate union of Jesus and our body and soul. The best way to prepare for this intimate union of lives is to avail ourselves of God's mercy. We could spend hours in preparation to receive the Eucharist, and at times perhaps we will. Yet there is no greater way to come to receive the Lord than to be cleansed of whatever may stand in the way. Honestly, this should need no explanation. God reveals the depths of the riches of his wisdom and his incomprehensible judgments and unsearchable ways in the simple, beautiful words, "I absolve you of your sins."

The Sacrament of Orders

Perhaps you may remember a children's game called Telephone. One person comes up with a phrase that passes person-to-person until everyone hears the original message. The point of the game is to see how different the message becomes because of it passing from person to person. Usually, the more people that pass the message, the more different the conclusion is from the original.

Imagine if Christianity came to us this way. The saving words and works of salvation passed along person-to-person, vulnerable to the limitations or prejudices of those that receive them. Without a guarantee that the original words and works would remain intact through time, we could never know with any degree of certainty that we have received exactly what Jesus intended.

Yet this is precisely what many people think about Christianity. As result, some have tried to recreate a Christianity purified of the defects of man. Others cling to the words of Scripture alone, believing the weaknesses of men did not dilute Sacred Scripture. The problem with both approaches is what they imply about God. If Jesus could not guarantee the safeguarding of his words and works from weak, fallible, sinful men, then I personally would question whether he is truly God.

As the title of this book suggests, I like to keep things simple. If Jesus is truly the Son of God, then he has safeguarded the transmission of the Gospel. There is no need to recreate a pristine or primitive Christianity, although every now and then it may need reforming. Likewise, the words of the Bible alone do not constitute Christianity. After all, they are the product of men, translations far removed from the original languages.

I believe that Jesus did, in fact, guarantee the transmission of the Gospel (and we do read about this in Sacred Scripture). Through the Holy Spirit given to the apostles, Jesus ensured that they would have everything they needed to continue his saving ministry. Not only would they recall all things concerning him, but they would be able to carry out his saving works (John 14:26).

By the gift of the Holy Spirit, Jesus ordained the apostles; he ordered their lives to this singular purpose. They in turn did the same, namely ordain other men to carry on the transmission of the Gospel. By calling down the Holy Spirit and laying hands on chosen men, the apostles passed along everything they had received from Christ (see Acts 1:21–22, 1 Corinthians 11:23).

Jesus cares so much about the mission he undertook on behalf of the Father that he instituted a way for it to continue until his return in glory. Jesus did not come only for the people of the time and place in which he lived. He came for people of all times and all places. He therefore chose certain men as apostles, to share in his work and continue it, not only in his name but also in his person. Through the sacrament of holy orders, this apostolic ministry continues in the deacons, priests, and bishops of the Catholic Church.

This sacred group (*ordo* in Latin), exists to serve the needs of all those who have been baptized, to build them up and unfold the riches of the grace of their baptism. Christ acts through the men that have been ordained to this life of service, and effects salvation through them. It really is that simple. Christ guarantees that the weaknesses, vulnerabilities, and sins of these chosen men will not impede his plan to unite all people to himself. In my way of thinking, if Jesus cannot guarantee this, then Christianity would be a waste of time because it would be merely the work of men.

Fortunately, I know Jesus can! I know him to be the Son of God because he chose me to serve him this way and has given me the best life of anyone I know. I live a life I certainly do not deserve, a life that continually expands in unimaginable and breathtaking ways. Jesus has ordered my life for his purposes alone. This is precisely the way he created me to live. The priesthood was not one choice equal to any other; it was the only choice. The priesthood is exactly what God had in mind for my humanity, just like wheat and wine for the Eucharist. For me, there was no other choice. There has only ever been and only ever will be this choice. As undeserving as I am, as sinful as I am, as weak and fragile, I will keep choosing this every day of my life. As long as he does not give up on me (which he never will), then I will never give up on that to which he has called me (and there are times I have wanted to because I am so painfully aware that I am not worthy).

What keeps me clinging to my vocation as a priest is the memory of what initially drew me to the priesthood. It was the look on my pastor's face when he elevated the Eucharist. I wanted to see what he saw when he gazed upon the Sacred Host held up before the people. In my mind, I can still see his face, transfixed with serenity and love. I knew he beheld the Lord of glory, and I too wanted desperately to see him. How remarkable it is that every day for twenty-five years, I have.

That is why, at every Mass I celebrate, when looking upon the elevated Host I say, "My Lord and my God. Save me from all that prevents me from loving you," then the following litany: "Jodi and David, Mom and Dad, Elizabeth and Stephen, Nana and Papaw, Frank and Cindy, Kelleen and Lauren, Michael, all the places I have had the privilege to serve, Kealani, Haley Fran, Bobby, Chrsitian, Thomas Ivan, Adrian." When I hold up the chalice, I say to Jesus, "Do not let Stephen, Dan, or William close their hearts to your love. Increase my capacity to love you. Do not hold my sins against the people you have asked me to serve. I'm sorry that I fail you."

Of course, I know that the priesthood is so much more than one particular sacrament or all of them together. The sacraments are just an extra benefit of giving my life to Jesus in service to his people. The majority of my day consists of more than the half hour to an hour when I celebrate Mass. The priesthood is not reducible to the mere celebration of the sacraments, although they lie at the heart of ordained ministry.

The priesthood more accurately describes who I am, and not what I do. This is an important point. It is easy to mistake ordained ministry as a job or a function, and then to evaluate it according to other jobs, other activities, other functions. Many people do, thereby demanding impossible and inapplicable changes. Just as the Church is an institution unlike any other social or synthetic institution, so too the priesthood is unlike any other way of being in the world. The Church and the priesthood have Christ as their origin. The divine initiative therefore distinguishes the essential elements of what defines them. While there are nonessential elements that can and have changed over time, the essential elements cannot. In terms of the priesthood, this means that it is exclusive to human males.

Once again, I need to say that either Jesus knew what he was doing, or he did not. To argue for a middle ground is really to suggest that Jesus is not the Son of God. If men have messed up what Jesus intended, then it would seem that men are more powerful than God is, and such a claim as that is absurd. Cultural norms did not limit and determine how the early Church established itself as a body; the plan of God did. The Holy Spirit made sure of this.

Jesus constituted the ordained ministry as the proper and fullest way for people of all times to experience his saving ministry. Sure, it is easy to think of this as a far-fetched claim, to demand greater inclusivity and social equality. It would be more fashionable to adapt to the changing whims of modernity, to adapt to relaxing mores and reductionist tendencies. Would not the God of love want such an adaptive loosening of what many perceive as archaic structures?

No. This way of thinking fails to recognize the divine acting within the human sphere. God's ways are not our ways, and our ways are not God's ways. At the heart of Christian discipleship is the willingness to die to self. We bend our will to the will of God and not vice versa. There are certainly many women whose gifts outshine the gifts of ordained men. However, it is important to remember that the talents of the person are not what matters. It is the plan of God that matters. Any argument claiming "of course men would say this" is once again implying the incompetence of God.

For the record, as a priest, I have no great power, at least not as the world conceives it. For instance, for twenty-five years I have lived as a Catholic bachelor. I cook my own meals, wash my own clothes, and clean my own bathroom (which I hate, and for which many souls leave purgatory). I have no say over anyone's life, other than to try to help them come to accept and experience the depths of God's love. I barely have control over my life, let alone another person's life. Yes, I can celebrate of the sacraments (except holy orders), but the majority of my life is not lived doing so. Like all of you, I spend most of my life trying to yield more of myself to the God who loves me. Jesus said the greatest among us must be the servant of all. Anyone that sees ministry in the Church from the perspective of power is, in my mind, automatically suspect.

I live my life of faith, my life in the Church, on the local level. No one in the Roman Curia cares what I think or knows that I even exist. I have never met Pope Francis, and most likely, I never will. I have almost no contact with the hierarchy, even though I am an extension of it. People, for many understandable reasons, have unrealistic criticisms of the Church. They argue against an abstraction and fail to recognize just what Church means within the context of their daily lives.

They should, of course, as an act of charity, point out our failures, weakness, and sins. This, the members of Christ's body must always do. We priests exist to help the riches of baptismal grace continue to unfold, but those whom we serve have an obligation to call us to accountability in terms of that for which Christ has ordered our lives. We need one another, but God has not created us in a way that we can all do the same things. Although the body is one, it has many members (see 1 Corinthians 12).

Bishops, priests, and deacons make up the smallest part in the body of Christ, yet they exist to serve the entire body. Together, we are all part of something greater than we are, something mystical but real. Knitted together, we incarnate the presence of Christ, bringing the love of God into the concrete conditions and circumstances of our lives. God has called us to this task. It is imperative that we support, encourage, and nourish one another in carrying it out.

To this end, wherever I go, I teach people how to pray for me. Whenever they put themselves in God's presence, I ask them to say simply, "Gary, Gary, Gary." I just want them to whisper my name to God. They do not have to ask for anything. God knows which Gary it is, and he knows, too, how in need I am of prayers as I continue serving him as a priest.

THE SACRAMENT OF MARRIAGE

I absolutely love presiding at weddings. I have been a priest for twenty-five years and have witnessed over 180 weddings. Although it is common for people to say, "Father so-and-so married us," I have never married anyone. Catholic priests do not marry the bride and groom; they only witness on behalf of the Church. The bride and groom marry each other.

Some priests find weddings to be a pain, but I certainly do not. (In fact, I do not find the celebration of any of the sacraments to be a pain.) I love the sacraments of the Church—all of them. Yet there is something special about the sacrament of marriage. It is as special to me as the Holy Eucharist.

These two gifts of Christ are wonderfully related. Both become the means by which divinity flows into the world. On a personal level, perhaps because I am so selfish and such a coward, I am in awe over the fact that two people risk themselves and their lives on one another (trusting of course, in God's help). It is always a privilege for me to be present with the family and friends the couple gathers to witness their love. I find my role as witness to be just as solemn as my role of presiding over the Holy Sacrifice of the Mass.

What makes this moment so special, so intensely sacred, is that all those present observe the fulfillment of the words Jeremiah shared with his people centuries ago. Through the union of their lives and the expression of their love, couples will "no longer have the need to teach their friends and relatives how to know the Lord" (Jeremiah 31:33–34). On their wedding day and beyond, the lives of the bride and groom become the lesson.

Many people—including Catholics—have misconceptions about just what takes place at a wedding. They erroneously think the couple comes to receive something from the Church, namely the sacrament of marriage. Yet that is far from the case. Couples do not stand before the Church's minister and the company of their family and friends to receive something. Rather, they are present on their wedding day to *become* something. Through their consent and the exchange of vows, the couple actually become the sacrament! It is not something they receive from the Church.

Through the grace that flows from the cross of Christ and by the action of the Holy Spirit, the covenant of the couple's love becomes a real, flesh-and-blood expression of the God that longs to have the least and the greatest know and experience how much he loves them. Married couples are not simply a sign of this; they truly become the means of communicating God's love, his grace, to the world. Just like the Holy Eucharist.

Jesus told us to love one another. What else better fulfills, ennobles, uplifts, and expands the human heart? Jesus exhorted us to love as he loves by laying down our lives for others. Through the sacrament of marriage a man and woman become the embodied expression of this commandment.

Every couple comes before the Lord because they have chosen the "still more excellent way" of which St. Paul speaks to the community at Corinth (1 Corinthians 13). On their wedding day, every couple is publicly expressing their desire to live a life of excellence! They want their love, the covenant they establish, the efficacious sign of God's presence they become, "to hope all things, believe all things, endure all things." They do not expect it to fail. On their wedding day, the couple affirms that they are not content with a life of mediocrity. That is why the company of friends and family is so important. In order to strive always for excellence, the couple will need help.

Of course, the nobility of what takes place may seem in the view of the world to be so unrealistic. The sacrament the couple becomes is risky; it entails tremendous sacrifice and self-denial. Yet great lovers know love is a risk, they know that fundamentally it is a choice that's made over and over again each day, often over and against what other people say, think, and perhaps advise. They also know that love is the greatest risk worth taking. On their wedding day, every couple sets their hearts on the higher things, choosing to risk everything on each other because they believe with all the holy ones that love never fails.

For Catholics, the celebration of a man leaving his father and mother and being joined to his wife is an opportunity for the couple to teach those they love the most—their family and friends—the truth about what is taking place. On their solemn and sacred day, the couple have the chance to speak to everyone gathered from the deepest recesses of their hearts through the prayers and Scripture passages they have selected.

The bride and groom invite others not only as witnesses of their love, but also as protectors. The celebration of the liturgy reminds those present about that which should matter most, the secret that makes us most fully and truly ourselves: Love one another.

On their wedding day, each bride and groom in a true and fitting way take the tabernacle into their home. Through the sacred character of the Church's solemn rite, the bride and groom show with their lives how the dignity of what they are undertaking is rooted, above all else, in the mutual, fruitful, exclusive, reciprocal exchange of themselves to each other. Through hospitality and genuine concern for others, the love between man and wife becomes a living, breathing sign that the Lord has truly given them everything in Christ.

Therefore, the Church honors and safeguards the sanctity of marriage. From the moment of birth, we cry out for the God who is love. We long for someone to hold, comfort, and feed us. We long to know that we are not like Adam, alone (see Genesis 2:18).

Each bride and groom, by the union of their lives, silence that first, instinctual cry by promising to each other, "I will comfort you; I will feed you; I will care for you. Your life is special, your life is meaningful; I believe in you! I love you! You will always be mine and I yours."

The secret to a long, fruitful married life is clear. As long as the couple believe that the Lord will never forsake or abandon them, then they will always be content with what they have, each other. This alone will not only enrich them, but everyone they meet and all those that make up the tapestry of their life together.

Instinctively we all know that married life teaches us the truth about being happy and at peace. It teaches us to fight against the desire to say, "This is as loving as I'll ever be, as patient as I'll ever be, as generous, attentive, responsive and as kind as I'll ever be. This is as good as I'm ever going to be."

When I witness the love of a bride and groom, I believe that I can be more loving, more forgiving, more attentive to others and more responsive to their needs. I know that I can overlook the silly and insignificant things that too often prevent me from truly being myself, that I can overlook wrongdoing and put my own interests aside. I know that with the grace of God, love is being perfected in me. Every wedding I have ever attended instills hope in me. Every bride and groom remind me that love must continue because love is the glory of our humanity fully alive! They know this because they have experienced this truth in one another. I know this from looking upon them, as they become a sacrament.

No one should ever seek to separate what God does in uniting a man and woman. They give themselves to God and to each other so that God can give them to us and to the world—as a gift. As a living, flesh-and-blood, body-soul-and-spirit sign and instrument of God's presence in the world, married couples offer us the chance to experience God gazing into our lives—through, with, and in them—whispering the words we all want and need to hear, "You are mine! You are special! I believe in you! I love you!"

The world needs the sacrament each married couple becomes. The eyes of the world look hopefully to them, for the union of their lives is a sure and steadfast sign that love never fails, that the Lord has set our lives as seal on his heart (see Song of Songs 8:6–7).

Last year, my parents died, approximately ten hours or less apart. They were married nearly fifty-nine years. My father raised his children, telling us repeatedly that meeting my mother was the greatest thing that ever happened to him, that he did not deserve her. He would say, "I knew her before any of you, and I will know her after all of you have left. She will always come first, and she is always right." We would cringe every time he went through this litany. It was not until I was older that I began to appreciate his words and recognized the impact they have upon my life.

My mother was the true love of his life and vice versa. As she slowly lost her mind to Alzheimer's, he made us promise they would stay together. For the last five years of my father's life, he could not care for her because he was bedridden, crippled from a neurological disorder. His mind remained intact throughout, but his muscles atrophied, his head dropped down, and his strength ebbed. The last two and half years of his life, he could not feed himself and lived mostly on chocolate ice cream and tapioca pudding (he had difficulty swallowing).

It was not an easy thing to do, but we kept our promise to my father. He and Mother remained at home—with twenty-four-hour nursing, until my mother's condition necessitated moving them. We found an innovative new approach to elder care that would allow them to live together in the same room. The decision weighed heavily on my father and was especially difficult for my eldest brother, who had oversight of them.

By the time they arrived, my mother was not able to recognize her children. She mostly thought of herself in the past and would talk incoherently about her "mamma and daddy." She thought she worked at the house they lived in and would tell me she could go down the street to her house whenever she wanted. She would also ask me if I knew Gary.

The last time she asked was not long before she died, and once again, I told her, "Yes, he's my best friend."

My mother said, "He's so busy with all his children. He has so many I don't know how he does it. He just loves his children. Will you see him?"

I said, "Yes Nancy, and I know he loves his children. He tries to take such good care of them. Did you know that his children and my children are all friends? They all grew up together, and we are both so proud of them."

That made my mother happy.

My father died first, which we expected. We hoped that my mother would not continue in her diminished condition for too long after. The day my father died, in some mysterious way, my mother knew she had a connection with "the man in the bed." She called him her "Lovie-do." His death and presence in the room rendered her inconsolable. It took my sister some hours to lovingly calm her down and eventually get her to sleep. When the nurse came in to the room early the next morning to check on her, the nurse discovered that my mother had passed sometime during the night.

My mother and father died the way they lived, totally for each other. I think when my father met Jesus he said, "I'm sorry, but I can't do this without Nancy." I think Jesus said, "Well, Frank, why don't you go and get her?"

THE SACRAMENT OF THE ANOINTING OF THE SICK

In October of 1999, I nearly died. In June of that year, I had begun a new assignment. The bishop warned me before I accepted the position that it was not going to be easy (which was an understatement). After being there for two months, I called him on the phone to tell him, "I think this assignment is going to kill me." It almost did.

The underlying problem I encountered when arriving had to do with the folks that had taken control of the ministry. A center established to attend to the spiritual needs of college students had become a private parish for more mature, disaffected Catholics. There was scant ministry to the students; thus, few had anything to do with the place. The previous priest director had given up trying to work out a compromise with this immovable obstacle. He had even hired a mediator in an attempt to make things more amenable to the students.

My first Sunday there, I reminded the members of this special community that the primary purpose of my ministry was the young people across the street. I told them they would be welcome on Sundays but that all programming—including liturgical ministries—would now be student-centered. They were not happy. One couple wrote to every bishop in the United States demanding my removal, claiming I had deep psychological problems. Another couple met with me to tell me how things were going to be. Another member told me I was "a Prince of Darkness, a bulldozer destroying the beauty of what we have created here."

The bishop shared with me every nasty letter he received that summer. I never imagined that people of faith could be so cruel. The more I made good on what I told them that first Sunday, the angrier and more vicious they became.

By the beginning of the semester, my health began to decline. I assumed it was just nerves, so I ignored how I was feeling. All the students had returned, and a few were slowly accepting my vision. My health worsened, so in the middle of September, I saw my doctor.

After examining me and asking me questions, she prescribed prednisone and Xanax. The pain continued to intensify, but the prednisone made me feel like I was Superman, and the Xanax knocked me out at night. This strange combination merely masked my true condition. On a number of occasions, my doctor drove down and injected me with meperidine.

In the midst of this increasingly painful and confusing time, I drove a group of students to Washington, DC. We went on pilgrimage to the Basilica of the National Shrine of the Immaculate Conception and the convent of the Missionaries of Charity, where I had cared for people with HIV/AIDS. I thought that the trip would help us bond. My administrative assistant, Pam, wisely counseled me not to go. Although I should have listened to her counsel, I went anyway. It was my first trip with the students, and I did not want to let them down. Big mistake!

I do not recall much of the trip, except the night I yelled at them to be quiet. (I know, not a good way to win their favor.) The Sunday we left, I told Megan, the other driver, "You'll have to drive the entire way home. I am going to double up on my pain meds and hopefully get some sleep."

By the grace of God, Megan's driving, and the students' nonstop praying (I was passed out), we returned to Illinois. The following day, in a fit of piety, I decided to stop taking my pain medication and offer up my suffering. This lasted but one day. I was in such pain I could barely function. I asked Pam to find me a new doctor. She knew there was something seriously wrong with me and searched for an internist willing to take me in that day. If not, she was taking me to the emergency room.

Pam found a Catholic internist who agreed to see me only because I was a priest. He was not taking new patients, so I would have to wait to see him until he had seen all his other scheduled patients. Late in the day, I drove myself to his office (against Pam's wishes) and was told I could wait in an examination room. The doctor would see me when he was finished with his last patient.

A nurse led me to a room and left. I leaned against the table and began praying my rosary (sitting caused me excruciating pain). I do not recall how long I waited because I was talking with Our Lady. That was enough for me. When the doctor opened the door of the examining room, he took one look at me and said, "Oh, Father, hospital, now." He did not even examine me. His receptionist drove me to the nearby Catholic hospital, and approximately eleven hours later, I was in surgery.

I was scared. I had never been hospitalized. When I phoned my parents to tell them what was happening, my mother told me to pull myself together.

"You'll be fine," she said.

I asked if they would fly out.

She said, "No. We will come and see you when you are out of the hospital."

My mother's words calmed me down because she was so certain that I would be fine.

It took a few tests for the doctor to diagnose me. I had a perforated abscess in my descending colon, and it was poisoning my blood system. When he told me I needed immediate surgery, I told him I needed a priest to anoint me. I was not about to undergo the first surgery of my life without allowing the Lord to lay his healing hands upon me. I knew that Jesus was with me, but I needed him to be tangibly present. I phoned a priest friend, and he dropped everything to come to the hospital and anoint me.

When my priest friend laid his hands upon me, I felt the same touch I felt when I was nine years old. Jesus was reaching out to me once again. I was just like all those I remember from his public ministry: men, women, and children to whom he extended the healing and comforting of the divine. The Lord's touch was nothing like the times I hold the consecrated host. It radiated throughout my entire body and generated such a profound calm and abiding peacefulness. The thoughts of weakness, of anguish, and of mortality fell away. I knew Christ was making my suffering his own, and that in turn taught me more about his.

Through the holy anointing, Jesus continues his ministry of healing and of forgiving sins. He meets those who are ill in the depths of their worry and pain, transforming the person's suffering by conforming it to his own passion and death. This mystical exchange unites the one suffering with the one who suffered for our well-being and redemption. This touches the very depth of the soul and may even flow out from there to heal the body. By the grace of the Holy Spirit, the one touched by Christ in the sacrament receives the courage needed to face the difficulties that serious illness and advanced age bring.

I know the sacrament to be exceptionally significant to those who suffer. Not just for the person that is ill, but likewise for the family. I witnessed this many years ago, the last time I asked Jesus for a favor (I personally never ask Jesus for anything. Petitionary prayer is not my thing. Jesus knows exactly what I need and daily provides for me).

My best friend's brother, Johnny, was in a coma and dying from leukemia. I knew Rob's entire family had gathered at the hospital, and I was keeping them all in my prayers. One day, while I was praying in the chapel of the Newman Center at Bradley University, I sensed Johnny interrupting my prayer, saying, "Come and see me."

Johnny was not Catholic, so I thought it odd that he insisted that I visit him in the hospital.

Talking like this may seem odd to some of you, but I learned from Mother Teresa that we should be attentive to those who reach out to us in the Spirit or through their guardian angels. Because Johnny would not leave me alone, I decided to end my prayer time. When I came out of the chapel, Pam asked me if everything was all right. I shared with her what had happened in the chapel, and she said, "Well, if he wants you to come and see him, you should go." I was thinking I should, but the hospital was over three hours away and I had to teach class in the morning.

I decided I would go, but just to be sure it was the right thing to do, I phoned a priest that I respected and asked him. I knew he would not think it weird that Johnny interrupted my prayer time. My friend instructed me to go, so I got in my car and headed to Madison, Wisconsin.

On my drive up north, I told Jesus, "You know I never ask for anything, so I'm calling in a favor. Johnny and his family need more time. I am not asking that you heal him, I am just asking for more time."

When I arrived at ICU, my friend Rob and his wife were not present. Rob's younger sister, Barb, told me that he and Tracy were in the cafeteria. Barb was shocked to see me, as was her sister Karen. I told them why I was there, that Johnny interrupted my prayer and asked that I come and see him. Johnny's parents were in the room with him, so Karen graciously took me into the room. Karen was not Catholic either, so I am sure this was a bit strange to her.

I had met Johnny's parents before. They knew I was a Catholic priest and their son Rob's friend. I told them what I had told Barb and Karen, that while I was praying, Johnny kept telling me to come and see him. I asked them if they would mind my praying over him. They were grateful I had come and warmly accepted my offer to pray.

Before I did, I bent down to speak to Johnny. I said into his right ear, "Johnny, it's Father Caster. Well, you got me here."

With that, he opened his eyes and turned his head toward me. His parents were dumbfounded.

I smiled at him and said, "Do you mind if we pray over you? I am going to lay my hands on you, and we will pray silently together."

Johnny nodded his head yes and closed his eyes. I invited his parents to lay their hands on him, which they did, and we all prayed in silence. When the room filled up with deep peace, I knew my time there was finished. The three of us walked out of the room and Johnny's parents thanked me for coming. I said goodbye to Barb and Karen, and they asked if I was staying to see Rob and Tracy. I told them I needed to get on the road, and off I went. I had done what I drove up there to do.

Johnny lived another two years, and so he was able to work out the things that needed his attention. The family believes that moment of prayer allowed Johnny to get his affairs in order.

Through the anointing of the sick, the Lord makes himself present as a healer, offering comfort and peace. He cleanses those who suffer from their sins and unites them with his passion and death. In these difficult and trying moments, Jesus comes to us just as he promised us he would.

CHAPTER TEN

Devotions

And whatever you do, in word or in deed, do everything in the name of the Lord Jesus, giving thanks to
God the Father through him. (COLOSSIANS 3:17)

AT THE BEGINNING OF THIS book, I mentioned how important it
is to frame each day. I shared with you the five things I say each
morning. While it is imperative to tell the Lord that we expect
him to punctuate our day with signs of his presence, I think it
is just as essential that we punctuate God's day with signs of
our presence. (For the ultra-theologically minded, humor me). I
regard devotions as the most fitting way of doing this.

To be clear, I know that for God, "one day is as a thousand
years, and a thousand years as a one day" (see 2 Peter 3:8).
God exists outside of time but nonetheless is always present
to us in time. I know each day is, in a manner of speaking,
our day. Yet I find that thinking about punctuating God's day
is an intentional way of living in relationship with him. It is
our way of establishing a vibrant reciprocity between the Lord

and ourselves. This is a fundamental aspect of any healthy relationship. Moreover, I find it to be a much more positive and engaging way to express my life with God. Not to mention the fact that he takes great delight in hearing from me, in being suddenly surprised by a bursting forth of me, just as I am always delighted and surprised by the moments he bursts forth in my day.

Devotions are an essential dimension of the spiritual life. They allow for our relationship with God to be more than an intellectual affair, to be a true affair of the heart. They give expression to the religious sense innate in every human being. The forms of popular piety we choose should flow out of the time we set aside to be alone each day with the Lord and spill back into this precious time.

In the Catholic Church, there are numerous forms of popular piety. We are encouraged to find the ones that touch our hearts and nurture us as we continue following Christ. I would like to mention just a few.

THE ROSARY

This is perhaps the oldest form of popular piety. What began as a means of enabling people to participate in the Liturgy of the Hours quickly became so much more. People felt that the recitation of the rosary fostered a greater sense of connection with Our Lady, and therefore with her Son. People with little or no formal religious education found the rosary to be an invaluable tool in deepening their knowledge and experience of the faith.

I like to think of the rosary as a stopwatch. It measures out for us a specific amount of time to pause and reflect upon the lives of Mary and Jesus and the mysteries of salvation. The rosary gives us a chance to take a time out, to step away from what is happening in our daily life and commune with God. In the time it takes us to complete the circle, we have a chance to root ourselves in that which matters most: God's love for us as it was expressed in the life, death, resurrection, and exaltation of Jesus.

The recitation of the familiar prayers frees our minds to contemplate the mysteries we recite or on any other aspect of the faith that may come to mind. The mysteries assigned to each decade do not restrict us. They are points from which we step into the inner workings of the divine, plumbing the inexhaustible richness of his love. The rhythm and pattern of this popular devotion forms a soothing descant, the perfect background music, as it were, for our exploration of God's saving love.

We do not pray the words to please Our Lady. As I have said before, she does not exist in heaven waiting and hoping to hear her name mentioned. She does not run around to the other saints and angels boasting about how many times she hears her name. She is pleased we pray the rosary, but not because it has anything to do with her. It pleases her because of the opportunity it affords us to appreciate and understand more fully the depth of the Father's love for us. She has no need of our attention because she remains forever the lowly handmaid of the Lord. She wants us to be evermore intimately united with her Son, and she knows the rosary is a means to this end.

My mother taught my brother and me to pray the rosary when we were in the second grade. We would pray it together at night before we went to bed. It was not long before the recitation of the rosary became an important part of my spiritual life. I knew that I could pray it anytime and anywhere. By the fifth grade, the sorrowful mysteries were by far my favorite, and they remain so to this day. In fact, I could spend time with every rosary I pray (and often do) reflecting only upon the scourging at the pillar. I am learning to appreciate better the luminous mysteries, but I have a long way to go. The best thing is, I do not have to pray them ever, but I try to stay within the pattern of the Church's prayer.

I also find the rosary to be an extremely intimate form of prayer, so I prefer to pray the rosary by myself. Of course, as a priest, I do occasionally have to pray it communally, and it is a real act of love for me to do so. One of my favorite times to pray the rosary is at the beach, lying in the sun. The warmth of the sun reminds me of the warmth of Our Lady's love for us. I also like to pray the rosary when I run, whether outdoors or on the treadmill. It takes my mind off the fact that I hate running.

My younger sister was just the opposite. She really enjoyed praying the rosary with the people of the parish where she attended daily Mass, an old immigrant parish that is now closed. She would go there on her lunch hour early enough to pray with the mostly elderly congregants. They prayed the rosary like it was a race to the finish line. It drove me crazy (which pleased my sister).

The first time the leader gave a nod to my sister to lead a decade, she was so excited that she lost count. When she began the extra Hail Mary, they all turned and gave her a stern look. She loved it! When next they signaled her to lead, she did the same thing. It did not take them long to realize that this was her little thing; they loved it.

When she was dying, my sister planned her entire funeral in her journal. She even went so far as to tell the priest she asked to preach what he should say. Because she wanted the rosary prayed to conclude the visitation, she drew a rosary in her journal and indicated in which decade she wanted the extra Hail Mary said. When the priest she asked to lead the rosary saw the picture in the journal, he laughed and cried. It was so very much my sister.

The night we concluded the visitation, the entire company of folks from her daily Mass parish were there to pray the rosary with us. When Monsignor hit the extra bead, they all began to cry. After, when they were taking their leave, they thanked Monsignor and told him, "Raquel would have wanted it that way."

Repetitive prayer is a part of many world religions. Repeating a word or sound or phrase is a proven way to free the mind for higher thoughts. The beauty of the words we repeat in the rosary tether us to sacred Scripture. Realistically though, this way of punctuating God's day will not appeal to everyone. If it does not appeal to you, fine. That does not mean there is something wrong with you. It does not mean Our Lady will be mad at you (far from it, she loves you). Simply find something else. St. Teresa of Ávila said that if our devotions are not bringing us closer to God, we should toss them aside and find ones that will. See how easy it is to live life in the Spirit.

Eucharistic Adoration

When I was a young man, it was common for Catholic parishes to offer a weekly holy hour at which people could pray before the Lord present in the Blessed Sacrament. This time of prayer concluded with benediction. The priest, wearing a veil that covered his hands, would lift the monstrance and make the Sign of the Cross over the congregation. It was not the priest blessing the people but Jesus. My mother took us regularly and taught us how to spend this time in prayer. It was solemn and somewhat mystical because the lights were dim, and the smoke from the incense danced around the altar.

My mother told us that if we did not know what to say to Jesus, we should speak the names of the people we loved and cared about. I would lift up whoever came to mind and watch them rise, lifted on the fragrant smoke that swirled around the Lord. I still do this each week during the holy hour we have on campus. The rising smoke still captures my attention as it wafts around the Sacred Host. Whispering people's names to Jesus is my favorite way of praying for them.

Sadly, for some reason I will never understand, this popular way of praying all but disappeared. Not long after the Second Vatican Council, many priests discouraged people from praying this way. I imagine they saw it as outdated, part of the old way of doing things. Such a tragedy and terribly misguided.

One seminary I attended actually forbade Eucharistic Adoration. We were encouraged to move beyond the "static presence" of Christ in the Eucharist. Is that the dumbest thing you have ever heard? Is the presence of the Son of God ever "static"? How could anyone make such an unintelligent statement about the source and summit of Christian life and worship? It is possible the priests did not believe Jesus is truly present, body, blood, soul, and divinity, in the Eucharist. While I was at this particular seminary, my classmates and I would sneak into the room in which the tabernacle was kept (no, it was not in the chapel) and make a holy hour together. To avoid detection, we did this after midnight when everyone was in bed. Can you imagine a Catholic seminary forbidding men studying to be priests from praying before the tabernacle? Strange times.

Fortunately, many parishes have resurrected this intimate devotional practice. Some parishes have built chapels that are open twenty-four hours a day so people can come and abide in the presence of the Lord. Of course, you do not have to stay for an entire hour, but it is a wonderful way to punctuate God's day with your presence. He just loves it when we stop in to say hello. If you have never spent time this way and you do not know what to say, do what my mother told us to do: Whisper the names of all those you love.

Getting used to sitting still before the Lord can take some time. Remember, you are building a relationship that will last forever. When I introduced Eucharistic Adoration at the St. Robert Bellarmine Newman Center, only a handful of students were familiar with the practice. I needed to catechize the broader community before we actually held our first holy hour. That first night was difficult for many of the young people that participated. Sitting still for an hour was not easy. I think many came out of curiosity, but at least they returned.

One young woman, Elizabeth, found it difficult to sit still. This was a completely new way of praying, and she tried to throw her entire self into it. I suggested she bring a journal and jot down the things she wanted to share with the Lord. I hoped it might help ease her into quiet reflection.

Elizabeth fell in love with praying before the Lord this way.

One afternoon, the tornado sirens started blaring, and suddenly someone burst into the center. Pam and I left our offices to see who it was and what was happening. As we came out of the office, Elizabeth bounded through the chapel doors carrying the tabernacle! When I asked what she was doing, she said she wanted to save Jesus from the tornado. I assured her that Jesus would be fine and encouraged her to go quickly to the shelter. I took the tabernacle and returned it to the chapel. It is one of my fondest memories. Elizabeth's concern demonstrates a true, lively relationship with Christ. When she arrived, she, like many of her peers, did not have a deep understanding of the faith. Now, she and her husband go weekly to Eucharistic Adoration along with a group of young adults. Elizabeth loves our Lord. I think Jesus got a big kick out of her trying to rescue him.

If you stop by an adoration chapel, I think it is important not to bring something to read. First, get used to speaking with the Lord and sharing what is in your heart. As you become more accustomed to spending time with him this way, you may want to bring spiritual reading, reflecting with him on what you are reading. This can lead to the development of great spiritual resolutions. Just make sure not to ignore the Lord.

When I was newly ordained, a friend asked me if I would mind covering his parish holy hour, which they held every Wednesday night. I was happy to do so. A nice crowd gathered the night I went, and after I exposed the Blessed Sacrament and we finished singing *O Salutaris* they began praying aloud. It sounded like they were shouting at Jesus. One prayer followed another, with hardly a breath in between. They even threw in a few litanies. It was nonstop chatter. After about fifteen minutes, I could not take any more, so I shouted, "Shut up! He knows who he is. He does not need affirmation. How about just speak to him from your hearts." Not my finest moment. This is probably the reason I will never be a parish priest.

They were kind enough to do what I suggested (or were afraid of the crazy young priest). We finished the hour in silence and concluded with benediction.

The next day the pastor called and said, "Gary, did you really say, 'Shut up'?"

I told him I did, and I apologized to him.

He said, "I didn't call for an apology. I called to thank you. I have wanted to change things myself but have been afraid to do so."

Be Innovative

Although all forms of piety are subject to the judgment of the Church, it does not mean we cannot come up with our own. Many of the more popular devotions began as individual initiatives. Over time, the Church embraced them, like the Chaplet of Divine Mercy or the Devotion to the Sacred Heart of Jesus. The only limit to punctuating God's day with signs of our presence is our imagination. I thought I would offer a few examples to illustrate the point.

Whenever I go shopping, I park as far away from the door as possible. Not only is it good exercise, it also offers me the chance to pray. With every step, I say to myself the name of Jesus, then Mary, then Joseph. Sometimes I make it a litany of the saints, so I say the names of all my friends in heaven. I also do this when I walk across campus.

I have also found an easy way to pray while I am driving. Whenever I see a Toyota 4Runner, I say a Hail Mary for

someone I wronged years ago. When I see a Lincoln, I pray for
the Bearce family. They welcomed me as one of their own since
I had no family in Peoria. Whenever I see a bird of prey, I say
a Hail Mary for my friend Rob. He is a convert. He took the
name of the apostle John when he came into the Church. When
I see something beautiful in nature, I say, "Blessed be God,"
and usually ask him how he does it. When I see horses, I say a
prayer for Coach and his wife. Ted would call me up when he
was free, and we would meet at the off-track betting site. When
I see a body of water, I say a prayer for my Christian hero Brian
and his wife and family. Yes, I have a Christian hero. I think
everyone should have a Christian hero or heroine.

Prayer should come naturally to us. Punctuating my driving
or walking by lifting my mind and heart to God makes it so
much more engaging. I think there would be no road rage if
we all drove on the lookout for something that would move
us to prayer. I know it has made me a much more patient and
more charitable driver. My friend Jodi takes a saint with her
whenever she goes to Walmart. You will be surprised how these
simple acts of piety will change you.

Sometimes the Lord himself will lead us to a devotion that will
speak to our hearts. This happened to me while in the seminary
at Rome. My vocation director and his assistant came to visit,
and after they left, I discovered that the assistant had placed
a prayer card in my breviary. On the front was a picture of
the Little Flower, and on the back was a prayer. At the bottom
of the card, the assistant wrote, "Say one for me please, Gary.
David." Therefore, I did, and I have been doing so for thirty

years. (Not only does David not know this, but he also does not like me).

The summer following their visit, I was back in Illinois, and one of the seminarians I was working with found the prayer card in my breviary. He wrote, "Me too, Ben." Somehow, word slowly went around, and I began finding prayer cards tucked into my breviary. They are in many different languages, and I have received them from bishops, priests, deacons, religious sisters, and many laity. Many of the people have long since passed from this life to the next, but I still say the prayer for them. Each morning when I conclude my own heart-to-heart with Jesus, I go through my cards. David's is, of course, the first one I pray. It takes me about twenty minutes to move through them, but I do not mind at all. I feel connected to all the people that had found a place in my breviary. I did not come up with this devotion; the Lord brought it to me through David. It is a vital part of my life with God.

While leading a mission in New Mexico, I did a show-and-tell with my prayer cards. After my conference that evening, a man my age, Greg, suggested I laminate them. The next day, we went to the bank where he worked and did so. He was concerned that my handling would damage them. He has since died, but Greg is with me every morning when I pray.

By sharing some of the things I do, I am not suggesting you do the same things. I merely want to show you how easy it is to stay connected with the Lord between the times we spend with him in reflective, meditative prayer. I also hope it encourages you to be creative, to think outside the box, to let your mind go wild. Start small. Once or twice a day, reverently make the

Sign of the Cross. This is a beautiful prayer. When you see a first responder, make the Sign of the Cross. When you see a funeral procession, make the Sign of the Cross. When you pass by a Church, make the Sign of the Cross. When you see a school bus, make the Sign of the Cross.

CHAPTER ELEVEN

Our Lady

Mary said, "Behold, I am the handmaid of the Lord. May it be done to me according to your word." (LUKE 1:38)

CHRIST DID NOT COME INTO the world in order that we might be one with him alone. He came into the world to gather all women and men to himself. It is impossible to follow Christ fully without a lived relationship with the company of his friends. We know this on a human level, for when we love someone, we are eager to meet his or her parents, siblings, and friends. As a man, Christ longs to share with us the relationships that are important to him, especially that of his mother and earthly father, Joseph. Neither Mary nor Joseph are incidental to the story of salvation or addendums to the life of Jesus. They spent more time with Jesus than any other men and women. In fact, Mary's assent to the Father's task for her life enables the Son of God to be born into the world.

Therefore, I cannot imagine a rich, exciting spiritual life without a close relationship with Mary. Jesus gave her to the Church on the day he suffered and died, and that is good enough for me. I have welcomed her into my life just as the apostle John did. As unworthy as I am, I want her to have space "under my roof," I want her to fill my life with the memories of her Son, which she holds in the depths of her heart. I need her maternal presence in my life, her wise counsel, her graced encouragement. I need someone I can turn to when my own lowliness is too much for me to bear. I need her when I feel as if my life cannot magnify anything but worthlessness.

I learned this when I was a boy. Reading about the apparition in Fatima was extremely moving. What most stood out to me was the fact Mary appeared to children. I know this probably seems funny, but I actually thought she might appear to me. I spent one summer sitting in the corner of my backyard waiting for her to appear. My mother would call me in for lunch telling me that Mary knew I needed to eat, but I would return afterwards to the same spot. You know, of course, she never came. It did not upset me; it just drew me closer to her. I would ask what I needed to do for her to come visit me.

While I did grow out of this (well, for the most part), I did not abandon my relationship with Jesus's mother. I grew closer to her and immersed myself in learning about all the apparitions the Church approved. This made me feel closer to her, and so, when I moved to Europe before entering the seminary, I decided to visit some of these remarkable places. Unfortunately, I never made it to Fatima, and yet I knew that someday I would make it there.

Long before that happened, I was finally accepted into the seminary. My third stop along the way to ordination brought me to Rome. The house was, at the time, very divided, liberals against conservatives, with a conservative ascendancy. I wanted none of this and still have difficulty understanding the Church divided into contemporary political factions. I love Christ and I love his bride the Church. My faith is that simple. I do not have any desire to change the Church, to make it more along the lines of what was or what it should be. I just want Gary to change into the man God created me to be.

Since I refused identifying with one camp or the other, I spent a majority of my time by myself. I would walk to class alone, when I went, and spent as much time in the city as possible. I went to St. Peter's Basilica as much as possible and Eucharistic Adoration at a different church nearly every day.

Keeping to myself proved to work out well for me, because in November of 1989, I learned the Berlin Wall might come down. The possibility of the destruction of this edifice to communism resonated so well with the messages from Fatima some seventy years before. I knew I had to be present for this historic moment. Therefore, I left the seminary and went to Berlin. I was away for ten days, and no one even realized I had been gone. I returned with pieces of the wall, which remain cherished possessions.

Throughout my years as a priest, I have shared this story with all my students; in fact, I share all my stories. I find that it is important for the people whom I serve to know something of me. I am no better than any of those I have had the privilege of serving; in fact, most of them are so much greater than I will ever be.

While serving at the St. Robert Bellarmine Newman Center, the students asked if we might go on pilgrimages together. I was overjoyed, as I never imagined they would want to travel anywhere with me. We had truly remarkable experiences traveling to many important and moving holy places. When I knew it would be my last year serving them, I asked if they would consider going to Fatima. I knew I was imposing my will, but they all offered an enthusiastic yes. At last, I could fulfill my hope to journey to this special place.

We arrived in Lisbon in the evening, and before driving to Fatima, we went to the home of St. Anthony for Mass. We arrived in Fatima late and settled in. We were scheduled to celebrate Mass early the next morning in apparition square, so everyone went to bed. The next day, before sunrise, we made our way on foot from the hotel to the square.

Everything was magnificent, including a flock of white doves that flew around the outdoor chapel after the consecration. One of the young men who assisted at Mass is now a priest. When Mass was concluded we took a quick walk through the square and I got in trouble for sitting in the chair used by St. John Paul II. After our brief tour, we made our way on foot back to our hotel for breakfast.

While walking back, one of the students began to scream. I was at the end of our group and ran immediately to the front to find out why this young woman was screaming, "Father, Father!"

When we caught up to her she was standing in front of a large chunk of the Berlin Wall enclosed in glass.

I asked her what was wrong, and she said, "Father, look! Look at the wall."

This I did, only to see that almost directly in the middle of the six-foot-by-four-foot chunk of the Berlin Wall was—in large black, block letters—the name, "GARY." The young woman that had noticed this said, "Father, Our Lady is welcoming you here! She is really glad you came."

By this time, the entire group had gathered around this monument to the defeat of communism, some asked if I had written my name on the wall, which of course I had not done. Even if I would have, the odds against it being the chunk that came to Fatima were astronomical. All I can tell you is that Our Lady finally did appear to me. We all took pictures of me standing in front of it pointing at my name. I keep the picture in my Bible.

Although the Church does not require any member to have a close relationship with Our Lady, I do not think the Church should have to. For me, being close to Our Lady makes perfect sense. Opening my life to her was as easy as opening my life to her Son. Since I was a boy, I have had endless conversations with her, asking not only for her guidance, but also for her comfort. Mary is with me right up to the end of my days. Then, she will introduce me to her Son, and my joy will be complete.

Mary's life is of course, a great model of the Christian life. I have found that different stages of her life reveal important dispositions that should emanate from every follower of Christ. I would like to mention them briefly, to encourage you to make space for Mary to dwell within your life as you follow her son.

BEFORE THE CONCEPTION OF JESUS: ANTICIPATION

Before the angel Gabriel appears to Our Lady, Mary was part of the faithful group of Israelites that were anticipating the fulfillment of God's promises. St. Luke presents a real sense of this when, after the birth of Jesus, Mary and Joseph bring him to the temple. There, they meet a man that has been "awaiting the consolation of Israel" (see Luke 2:25) and a woman who "spent her days in prayer and fasting," awaiting the redemption of Israel (see Luke 2:38). Mary embraced the longing of her people, and with them, she believed God would be true to his word.

Her understanding of how this would take place was of course, shaped by her people's conception of Israel's redemption. They thought of it primarily in geographical, political, and religious terms. They knew that history matters to God, and so the historical memory they carried with them became the lens through which they viewed their future. Added to this expectant longing was an openness to that which they could not imagine. We see this openness in Mary when she listens to the angel and accepts God's plan for her.

At this time in her life, Mary demonstrates how anticipation is an essential Christian disposition. We must live with the expectation that God indeed will fulfill his promises in our lives. We must be open, like Mary, to that which we cannot conceive, that which seems beyond our capabilities. God will never force us to accept that which he asks us to do. Like Mary, at times, we will have to give our assent over and against what we feel, what we know, and what we desire. Like her, we must come to know our lives solely in terms of what God is up to for us, and therefore for others. We must be willing to yield to grace, willing to give to Christ whatever he needs from us.

DURING THE PREGNANCY: WONDER

I can scarcely imagine what those nine months must have been like for Mary. I have little doubt it must have been like a private, intensive retreat. Each day, she contemplated this life united with her own, growing day by day, needing her, depending upon her. Imagine the day she first felt Christ move within her. These nine months were such a privileged time for her, one that I think every woman that has been able to conceive understands.

A great sense of wonder overshadows Mary during this precious time. The child's divine origins infuse the natural feelings any expectant mother might have and instills within Mary a recognition of the way in which her life is being affected by the Holy Spirit. She knows the movement of the Spirit within her bodily life now so intricately bound with that of God's Son. She also knows the action of the Spirit within her emotional life, the hormones necessary for generating life now charged with the "grandeur of God." Is this not what her Magnificat is, a wondrous outpouring of spirited emotion (see Luke 1:46–55)?

Each day as the child grew within her, Mary was conscious of exactly what God needed from her. God did not simply need a womb; he needed Mary, the young maiden of Nazareth. The presence of the child growing in her womb, touching and transforming everything she knew about herself, about God, and about the world, taught Mary that God does not save souls; he saves the whole person. She may have been conceived without sin, but during these nine months, she understood salvation and redemption from an entirely new perspective, that of Christ.

Mary learned that the plan of God in our lives always touches that which is most personal. She anticipates well the words of St. Paul because she truly glorifies God in her body (see 1 Corinthians 6:20). Mary's interior life is not distinct from her bodily life. Her vocation influences the way she experiences life in her body. She did not rebel against what God needed from her, nor did she accept it with resignation. Rather, she welcomed the plan of God with determination and interior peace, and this in turn fostered that wondrous disposition which led her to say, "The Almighty has done great things for me and holy is his name" (see Luke 1:49).

BEFORE PUBLIC MINISTRY: AMAZEMENT

It is both remarkable and beautiful that Mary and Joseph, knowing Jesus to be the Son of God, continue to be amazed at what was happening around them. They were far from complacent. They remained engaged and struck by everything that took place as God's plan continued to unfold. St. Luke records their disposition with respect to the words of the shepherds (see Luke 2:18) and what they experienced in meeting Simeon and Anna in the Temple (see Luke 2:33).

Mary and Joseph were attentive to the fact that within the ordinary and expected aspects of their lives, the most extraordinary and unexpected things kept happening. The sense of wonder Mary had at the fact of the child growing within her distilled into an abiding sense of surprise concerning their vocation to raise the child Jesus. In addition, they were not alone. The angels of God sang to the shepherds and the heavens guided the magi to the child Jesus. God's plan is not static but is possessed of a dynamism that permeates the whole of creation.

The mother and father of Jesus did all that God required them to do and thus they discovered that they were not "lacking in any spiritual gift" (see 1 Corinthians 1:7). They remained attentive to their vocation even through the difficult, challenging, and confusing moments. By centering their lives on Christ, they discovered that his needs would be specifically determined. God was asking more of them than merely to provide a safe, loving environment for the child. He was asking that they lay down their lives for his Son. In doing so, they were the first followers of Christ to reveal Christian discipleship as the willingness to incarnate love in the concrete conditions and circumstances of life. They could do so because they had everything they needed. Love for Jesus pulled them through. Love for Jesus pulls us through.

DURING PUBLIC MINISTRY: CONFIDENCE

Mary's confidence in her Son's public ministry emerges early on in the Gospel of St. John (see John 2:1–12). At the wedding at Cana, where she is present, she notices that the wine has run out. One could write an entire work on the abundant, rich, and important imagery; I wish to point out just a couple of things.

First, because John begins the recounting of this event by mentioning Mary, her presence is a fundamental part of everything that follows. Jesus and the disciples seem almost an afterthought ("they were also invited"). Perhaps Mary knew the couple or their families, which is why she is particularly attentive to the details. Mary knows that wine, which God has given "to cheer and warm man's heart" (see Psalm 103:15), is an important part of the celebration. She also knows the reason her Son is born into the world: to cheer man's heart with the warmth of divine love.

When she presents the dilemma to Jesus, I think she has more in mind than taking care of social niceties. She, more than any other human being, best understands our need to be in a right relationship with God. The problem caused by original sin needs rectifying. A wedding is the perfect opportunity to show that God does in fact desire union with us. When she approaches Jesus with the problem of the wine, she does not need to elaborate. After nearly thirty years with her Son, she can say things to him with a look, a gesture, a simple phrase. Far from rebuking her, I find his comment to be a tongue-in-cheek moment between them. I imagine Jesus saying, "And what concern of this is mine?" with a knowing gleam in his eye. I know my mother could do the same with me, and sometimes I would impishly say, "What?"

That is the reason Mary turns to the stewards and tells them to do whatever Jesus says. She is so utterly confident that he will do something that she does not have to insert herself any further in the situation. Her selfless concern for others naturally leads her to her Son, whom she knows will give the couple whatever they really need. She is willing to share her Son with the couple because she knows it is time to take up the task for which he was born. Mary is willing to hand on to everyone present what she herself received, namely, the Son of God (see 1 Corinthians 11:23).

Mary is also willing to give Christ the freedom to do his work. This is exactly what confidence in God produces in the heart of the believer. We no longer seek to control or influence the way God acts. Rather, we know that God will act and always in the way that is best. This is the true freedom of being God's child. Mary knows that Jesus will bring his good work to completion, however he chooses. Her confidence casts out all negativity, worry, or doubt. Because she knows her Son so well, she knows that nothing is too small or insignificant to him. The fact that there is no more wine will matter to Jesus because it matters to Mary. This is confidence at its best.

AFTER DEATH AND RESURRECTION: CONTENTMENT

Some years ago, two Christian authors wrote a series of books entitled *Left Behind*. The story is rooted in an American Protestant exposition of St. Paul's First Letter to the Thessalonians, chapter 4, verses 13–18. Here Paul seeks to give encouraging words about the living and those who have died with respect to the return of Jesus in glory. While the speculations of the authors stand way outside Catholic teaching on the end times, they do overlook an important Scriptural fact. The only person that we can say with certainty that was "left behind" was Mary. If any follower of Jesus should have accompanied him to the right hand of the Father, I think it should be Mary. Scripture says otherwise. Mary did not ascend with Jesus; she stayed behind with the rest of his followers. After everything she had been through, there was yet more for her to do.

These years with the apostles and other followers of Christ crystallized her vocation. Her maternity was not just in bearing Jesus and raising him to manhood. Her maternity embraced the company of his friends. The early Church needed her, just as the Church does today. She was a repository of much wisdom concerning God the Father, her Son Jesus, and also the Holy Spirit. Who better to help them recognize and understand the working of the Spirit than the woman whose whole being the Spirit overshadowed? Who better to teach them how to wait for the coming of Christ in glory than someone that should not have to wait for him?

By her presence within the community, Mary embodied the truth that God shows no partiality. Waiting was not a punishment but an opportunity and an experience of redemption. I have no doubt St. Peter learned this from Mary. He writes in his second letter, "Therefore, be all the more eager to make your call and election firm, for in doing so you will never stumble." (2 Peter 1:11). Peter and the other apostles learned from Mary how to be content in their vocations, how to "keep [themselves] in the love of God and wait for the mercy of our Lord Jesus Christ that leads to eternal life" (Jude 1:20–21). Our Lady encouraged them to remember that our "citizenship is in heaven, and from it we await a savior, the Lord Jesus Christ" (Philippians 3:20). Who better to keep them centered in terms of their relationship with Christ than the woman who not only had been doing so, but also now would continue to do so?

One last important point: I think one of the great gifts of Mary's presence to the early Church has to do with the Eucharist. She was the only person that could help the followers of Christ understand this gift. Having received the Son of God into her physical body, she was able to guide those who were now receiving Jesus, body, blood, soul, and divinity, into their bodies. Mary best appreciates the overwhelming and beautiful means by which Christ remains with us until the end of time. I often think about what it was like for Mary receive her Son in the Eucharist and share with the Church in the sacramental life. Perhaps she discussed this with them as they grew to understand more fully what Christ entrusted to them. I know she continually helps me to do so. I know she longs to help you as well.

CHAPTER TWELVE

The Angels and the Saints

Therefore, since we are surrounded by so great a cloud of witnesses, let us rid ourselves of every burden of sin that clings to us and persevere in running the race that lies before us, while keeping our eyes fixed on Jesus, the leader and perfecter of faith. (HEBREWS 12:1-2)

THE CHURCH HAS LONG UNDERSTOOD that the community of Christ's body extends to those who have gone before us marked with the sign of faith. This body of the faithful therefore includes both the living and the dead, those awaiting fullness of life within the eternity of God's love, here (the Church militant) and in purgatory (the Church suffering), as well as those already beholding clearly God himself, Triune and one (the Church triumphant). As St. Paul reminded the Christians of Rome, "In one Spirit we were all baptized into one body" (1 Corinthians 12:13).

As members of the Church, we are not alienated from one another. Everyone who is of Christ and possesses his Spirit form one church and in Christ cling together. Even now, the living and the dead unite in a mystical communion that allows their relationships to not only continue, but also to deepen. The first preface for the Mass of Christian burial reassures those who mourn that "life has changed, not ended." Our hope for eternal life should therefore be more than a hope for reunion with our deceased loved ones. Our hope must center on experiencing the communion we already share without any limitations or imperfections. If the living have no access to the lives of those who have died, then Christ did not conquer death, and our faith is empty (see 1 Corinthians 15:12–19).

The Church's teaching on the communion of the saints assures us that our faith is far from empty. Through the power of the Holy Spirit, baptism unites us in a communion of love that "neither death, nor life, nor future things, nor powers, nor height, nor depth, nor any other creature" is able to destroy (Romans 8:38–39). We have died and risen with Christ! The only limits to experiencing the fullness of life that Christ offers are those we set for ourselves, in thought, in word, and in deed. To live fully the communion that Christ offers us as members of his body, we must be open to the rich treasury of his love. By an exchange of spiritual goods (CCC 947) and by our openness to the men and women who facilitate this exchange, we reinforce the communion Christ offers. Being receptive to the whole of Christ's body ensures being faithful to the deepest vocation of the Church.

Therefore, we should have friends of Jesus throughout our earthly journey, both in heaven and on earth. I depend upon the company of Christ's friends to challenge and support me, uphold me and celebrate with me, to keep me forever close to the one our hearts love. Living without the friends of Jesus imperils the spiritual life, because in the end, we are just following ourselves.

It is impossible to keep up the momentum to follow if we are only following ourselves. The saints in heaven and on earth help to keep our hearts rooted in Christ. We need both; at least, I know I do. The saints now in communion with Jesus are true and lasting friends that long to have us fully share with them the life and love of the Triune God.

I suggest that if you do not yet have a friend in heaven, besides the Lord, of course, find one. There are a multitude from which to choose. They are from every state of life and every century. They are male and female, young and old. Each of their stories is unique; no two are the same. I met my first heavenly friend at the suggestion of my fourth grade teacher. St. Thérèse of Lisiuex and I have been friends since then. She knows me so well and looks after me with such care. She also likes to joke around with me. She lived her life filled with confidence and love and has taught me how to do the same in my life. My first male heavenly friend is St. Claude de la Colombière. He was a Jesuit priest that worked in the court of the French king, tutoring his sons. After a brief and difficult time in London, he moved to Paray-le-Monial, France, as the confessor to St. Margaret Mary Alacoque. She was the cloistered sister to whom Jesus appeared, revealing his sacred heart. Like St. Thérèse, St. Claude also lived with confidence. His relationship with God was marked with such positivity that I knew we were kindred souls. I could write an entire book on the ways in which St. Claude has helped me understand my priestly life and embrace the universal call to holiness.

On November 21, 1964, Pope Paul VI promulgated the Dogmatic Constitution on the Church, *Lumen Gentium*. This foundational document of the Second Vatican Council presents the "deep vocation of the Church" in bold new terms, describing it as the means of promoting "a more human manner of living." An entire chapter is therefore dedicated to what the council fathers term "the universal call to holiness." Chapter five encourages the faithful "of whatever rank or status" to accept that the fullness of Christian life is not just for those who have renounced everything for the sake of the Gospel but also for all members of Christ's body.

This new articulation of an ancient truth provided a fresh perspective with which the faithful could view their lives. Those whose task it is to live and work in the world are encouraged to accept that achieving this perfection was truly possible. By trusting in the strength received from Christ, they could in fact follow his example regardless of "their condition, duties or circumstances." By seeking the will of the Father in all things, they would be ever more conformed to Christ's image. By remaining devoted to God and the service of their neighbor, they would ensure a "harvest of good." By accepting this universal call to holiness, they were accepting the truth that all members of Christ's body can become the saints Christ calls them to be.

Perhaps the foremost proponent of this great insight of the council was St. John Paul II. While the breadth and depth of his pontificate has made it truly historic, three unparalleled dimensions of his tenure underscore his commitment to this teaching: the extent of his writings; the overwhelming number of men and women he beatified and canonized; and the wide range of his travels. As the Vicar of Christ, John Paul II did all that he could to expand upon the council's insight, encourage people of good will of its veracity, and invite the faithful to embrace it enthusiastically.

Although his encyclicals, apostolic letters, homilies, and Wednesday audiences addressed a wide range of theological, philosophical, and sociological points, nearly all of them build upon the following conciliar theme: "Christ fully reveals man to man himself." Repeatedly, John Paul would use these words, reminding the Church that the possibility of living out the universal call to holiness depends upon a willingness to place the whole of one's life before the Lord. Within the light of this encounter—one not to be feared, we discover the truth of who we are and that which prevents us from being the man or woman God created us to be.

This revelation does not alienate us from God, but draws us into the Father's providential care. In the light of divine love, we are better able to carry out that which is distinctively human, building up society according to its divine end and increasing the solidarity of the entire human family until the day of its perfection. This revelation, an act of selfless love on the part of Christ, instills within the hearts of believers the conviction that they can become perfect "just as our heavenly Father is perfect" (see Matthew 5:48). Open to all that Christ reveals we can experience here and now, the unfathomable love the Father longs to lavish upon his children.

St. John Paul truly appreciated how discovering ourselves in God is the key to personal sanctity. Thus, he took a special interest in the men and women promoted as outstanding expressions of love for God and service to one's neighbor. Each solemn liturgy of beatification and canonization was an opportunity for the Holy Father to put a name and face upon the truth of the council's claim. For twenty-seven years, he presented to the world men and women of every age and from all states of life who had not been afraid to stand before the Lord and discover who they were. In celebrating their lives, the Holy Father gave us the chance to reflect upon our own and consider what is possible for those who are united to Christ. With each official declaration, he was proclaiming to the world that we, like the saints can love God passionately, abide in his presence and serve the world with charity. St. John Paul II knew this was the lasting hallmark of those who believe.

The large numbers he added to the Church's register of saints is wonderfully appealing. It should be an encouragement to all the baptized. Though the call to holiness is universal—the same for everyone, everywhere—we express it within the unique circumstances of our lives. St. John Paul introduced this vast company to the world as a lasting reminder that within the ordinary conditions of our lives we should expect the most extraordinary, seeing "the even greater things" that Jesus promised those who follow him (see John 1:50).

What was true for the men and women beatified and canonized by St. John Paul remains true for all members of Christ's body. Only in an encounter with Christ is our humanity able to communicate the love out of and for which it is created. Jesus facilitated such an encounter during his public ministry by traveling throughout Judea and Galilee. He stopped in towns and villages, making himself available in synagogues, public places, and private homes. Often, he returned to towns he had already visited so that others might have the chance to encounter him.

THE ANGELS AND THE SAINTS

St. John Paul II also made stops in towns and villages—all around the world. He returned frequently to places he had already been. John Paul II knew that, fundamentally, Christianity is an event, something that happens when the human heart encounters the Triune God. Within the first months of his pontificate, he resolved to help facilitate this event, and did so through his pastoral visits.

Throughout his pontificate, John Paul II would use his office as a kind of sacrament of presence, not just to the people of Rome and visitors to the Vatican, but to people all over the world, especially the young. His election as supreme head of the Church would be an opportunity for him to incarnate everything he believed, animating with enthusiastic hope the words of Jesus, "nothing is impossible for God" (see Matthew 19:26).

Through his travels, John Paul II was able to accomplish what words alone could not. Each trip became a chance for him to unite within the sights and sounds and gestures of the Mass the thoughts expressed in his letters and the love that stirred within his heart. The beauty of each papal liturgy would be for those open and receptive an opportunity to stand before the Lord and discover who they truly were. I think this is the reason why John Paul II would repeatedly tell the different groups with whom he met, "Be who you are!"

By making himself so available, many people were able to experience that which the Holy Father wanted for them. It is no wonder then that the multitude gathered for his funeral liturgy would cry out, "*Santo subito,*" demanding that the Church add him to the ranks of the saints. The faithful recognized that John Paul had lived the way he encouraged others to, that he had willingly placed himself before the Lord, that he had discovered who he was, and that he had accepted all the Father asked of him. The faithful appreciated that the sanctity of the man who served as the head of the Church was born of his desire to be their friend.

The whole company of men and women united in Christ and experiencing the eternity of God's love want precisely the same thing as Pope John Paul II: they want us to encounter Christ in such a way that our lives become open to the full, rich possibilities that exist within the mind of the Father. The saints want us to live within the light of the truth that only Christ reveals, experiencing now what it means to live the joy and freedom of the children of God. The saints do not *want* to be our friends; they already *are* our friends. From within the Trinitarian communion, they long to help us experience more deeply the inexhaustible splendor of God's love.

They do this first by helping us see more clearly who we are. They offer their lives as a mirror in which we can reflect upon our own. By granting them a place in our lives, they are able to point out ways in which we need to change, and they give us the encouragement to do so. Like any good friend, they stand by us, constantly assuring us that where they are, we might likewise be. They never condemn, belittle, or reject us.

Through, with, and in Christ, the saints are truly present to us. They are not merely figures from the past, and it is not their life histories that help us become holy. Nor do they exist on some higher plane to which we have no access. Christ brings us into communion with them so that we can accept and experience the gift of friendship he makes possible. By sharing fully in Christ's mission to unite all things in himself, they serve and glorify the Father. The saints do not hinder or replace the work of Christ; they subsist as a perpetual part of it. Their intercession is therefore more than just a prayer spoken on our behalf; it is a willed act of their whole being, directed at our salvation. This enables them to be effective in our lives like the friends who help us accept and understand things that others cannot.

The saints change our lives by the intellectual, emotional, spiritual, and yes, physical access we extend to them. They walk with us along our pilgrim journey, preventing us—literally and in real time—from stumbling and picking us up when we do. Like all good friendships, those with the saints enhance our lives because the relationship regularly pulls us out of ourselves, safeguarding us from all the ways in which we narrow, limit, or constrict our sense of what it means to be human. Their presence establishes a healthy and positive awareness of our humanity and the inherent dignity we possess in virtue of bearing the image and likeness of God. Being true friends with the saints is a sure safeguard against all the pernicious heresies that demean and devalue human existence.

The saints accomplish all of this just as Jesus did for the Samaritan woman (John 4:4–42). When he sat and spoke with her at Jacob's well, it was not to make her feel bad. Pointing out "everything she had ever done" was a necessary part of the encounter. The man asking for a drink of water knew the woman needed to have her life placed in relief. Jesus's presence, along with his words, acted as a catalyst for the woman to appreciate herself from a new perspective. This new and profound awareness was so incredibly freeing that the woman, without any thought as to what others might think, returned to her town enthusiastically announcing her discovery. The man at the well may indeed be the Messiah, for who but the Messiah could have altered and expanded her point of view?

The saints serve Christ because they also tell us everything we have ever done. Sometimes the way they go about pointing out our need to change is with humor, because laughter keeps the devil away. At other times, what they show us humbles us. Yet, no matter how the saints enable us to see our lives more clearly, it is indispensable that they do. All those who, like the Samaritan woman, remain steadfastly receptive know this experience to be always healing and refreshing.

What the saints do for us, while vital to our friendship with Christ, does entail a significant risk. Whenever Christ, the saints, friends, or strangers reflect our lives back to us, there is always a chance we will reject what we see. Jesus takes a risk by entering into conversation with the Samaritan woman, even though what he says is characteristic of a healthy and loving friendship. We should welcome in our lives those who not only want what is best for us, but also help us to see it. We should have as friends those who are willing to say even that which we may not want to hear. Good friends increase our self-awareness, encourage and support us, and never ask us to do anything hurtful or unhealthy. We should welcome in our lives all those who long to help us become the person God has created us to be. No one of us is ever above correction.

The woman at the well welcomed Jesus into her life and invited him to her home because she recognized the kind of friendship he was offering. Having tried and failed at satisfying the desires of her heart, the encounter with Jesus presents the Samaritan woman with a new chance to do so. However unlikely it may be, this man is offering her what no other man could. Jesus's presence stirs within her something so profoundly personal that she is unable to remain at the well. She leaves having already tasted the life-giving water he promises her, compelled to extend to the people of her town the friendship Christ has offered her.

The desire to invite others to share the experience of meeting Christ occurs frequently in the Gospels. Often, the Gospels present human friendship as an instrument of Christian discipleship. In the Gospel of John, Philip encourages his friend Nathanael to join him, using the words Jesus spoke to the followers of John the Baptist, "Come and see" (John 1:39). Nathanael agrees to follow most likely out of curiosity: "Can anything good come out of Nazareth?" (John 1:46).

Jesus does not disappoint Nathanael! Immediately, what Jesus says strikes Nathanael's heart. It hardly seems possible that a man Nathanael has never met could know him. Jesus builds upon Nathanael's curiosity, using it to accomplish the same thing as with the Samaritan woman. By the end of each encounter, both Nathanael and the Samaritan woman have been hooked by the fisher of men. Jesus's knowledge touches the deepest part of them in an entirely unexpected way: it satisfies the original desire of their hearts.

What is notable about the response each makes to Christ is their absolute willingness to accept that he does in fact know them. Although Nathanael does question the source of Jesus's knowledge, the Samaritan woman has little trouble with that which Jesus shares. All her life, she has longed for someone that understands, for someone who actually gets her. In this way, she is no different from any one of us. We all long to be known; we all long to have at least one person actually grasp who we are. That which is most intimately constitutive of our being calls out for recognition, and friendship answers this call.

Nathanael also learns this important lesson. Jesus's promise of "greater things" may entice him to remain, but it is the need to be known that enables Nathanael to continue following. Once we have discovered ourselves in Christ, it is nearly impossible to walk away. His words of everlasting life are so much more than theological insights and moral imperatives. They are words that uniquely and personally touch our hearts. Those "with ears to hear" find that the innate desires of the heart can be fully satisfied.

In the encounter with the Samaritan woman and with Nathanael, Jesus reveals divine friendship as the guarantee of human fulfillment. His promise of even "greater things" is secured by the infinite and unconditional love that fashioned and made us. While the initial momentum of Christian discipleship fosters a desire to be known, only Christ can sustain it. Once his words resonate within the depths of our hearts, the truth to which Jesus's testifies convicts it. Denying, abandoning, or rejecting the truth would be the same as denying ourselves. Once the words of Christ live in our hearts, we cannot ignore them. We may not always live up to the truth of who we are, but we can no longer pretend we do not know it. That which Christ awakens in our hearts never really goes away.

The saints constantly remind us of this. By encouraging us to be who we are, they help us to keep on following Christ.

By continually enhancing self-knowledge, they ensure that our relationship with Christ governs all the facets of our lives. Our friendship with them persistently renews our convictions, giving us the courage to stand unashamed in the light of Christ's love. Our ongoing conversation with them about the things they show us and the lessons they teach us fixes our gaze firmly on the person of Christ.

Their knowledge of our lives, after all, comes from Christ. As the mediator of the new covenant (see Hebrews 9:15), he allows the saints to help us receive our promised inheritance, just as he allowed Philip to help Nathanael obtain his. The saints are not all-knowing. Their knowledge of us originates in Christ and expands as our friendship with them grows. What they share with us, therefore, is never general and impersonal. They specifically direct their efforts toward the one who lets them in. My friendship with St. Claude will never be the same as someone else's. While there may certainly be similarities because the saints—like us—have personalities, fundamentally, the experience is uniquely ours.

As men and women who saw and experienced the "greater things" that Jesus promised Nathanael, they also draw our attention to the concrete circumstances and situations that reveal these greater things. Friendship with them is a great gift offered to us by Christ, an inherent part of the act of "revealing man to man himself" (Pastoral Constitution on the Church in the Modern World). The gift of their friendship corresponds perfectly to the goodness, truth, and beauty of our humanity, because their own humanity exists within the life of God. They do show us Christ, but they also show us everything we have ever done. The saints know best who we truly are.

Not only do the saints long for us to share fully in God's life and love, but so do the angels. These spiritual creatures exist to serve the Father. Since the Father longs to unite all people to himself, the angels actively and tirelessly work to achieve this end. We should therefore make room for them in our lives, calling on their assistance and joyfully and gratefully acknowledging their presence.

For generations now, the Church has encouraged her members to foster devotion to their guardian angels. I learned the importance of this in my spiritual life from Mother Teresa and her sisters.

One Sunday, the volunteer that regularly drove the sisters to their respective apostolates was unable to do so. After Mass, Mother asked Monsignor (now Bishop) Curlin if I was able to drive them. Of course, he told her yes, and so I went and got the fifteen-passenger van used for this purpose. I pulled it up to the front of the convent and waited while the six sisters entered the van. It was a lived Gospel moment, for two by two, the sisters would spend the day in service to God's people. They all took their seats, and I put the van in gear and proceeded down the long driveway.

Before we left the property and just as they started to pray the rosary, I asked them, "Sisters, where am I taking you?"

One of them called out in a quiet voice, "We do not know."

I slammed on the breaks. "Do you at least know what direction I should go?"

"No, brother," one sister responded, "because we keep custody of the eyes. We do not look out the windows."

"Sisters," I said, "how can I take you where you need to go if you do not know the way?"

"We will ask our guardian angels to tell your guardian angel where to take us."

Being relatively new to the ways of the Missionaries of Charity, I thought this was, honestly, a bit crazy. I was not yet a true believer! Nevertheless, I put the car back in gear and left the property.

Having no clue where to take them, the thought came to me that I should head toward downtown Washington, DC. The sisters continued praying aloud the rosary, while I drove the van asking my guardian angel for help. This was a first. I never talked to my guardian angel. I did say the children's prayer when I was young, but that was twenty plus years ago.

As we approached downtown, I had an impulse to turn right, so I did. I continued on a few blocks, made a left, then, further on, a right. I made these turns as if I knew what I was doing.

About a mile along, I made another right and instantly one of the sisters cried, "Brother, stop the van!"

We came to a screeching halt. Two sisters calmly exited the van and walked up to the front door of a brownstone. Two down, four to go.

Once more, I put the van in gear, and we continued on our way. I did what I had done before and turned whenever I felt like it. Although this did freak me out a bit, I also enjoyed the mystery of it all. Eventually, I was able to get each pair of sisters just where they needed to be. The last stop was at a hospital by Robert F. Kennedy Memorial Stadium. When the two sisters exited the van, one of them asked if I would be picking them up. I emphatically said no. I had had enough. My head was spinning. I had a lot of thinking to do.

When I returned to the convent, I put the van back in its place and walked to the front toward Monsignor's car. He and Mother were sitting by the fountain, no doubt talking about spiritual things. I walked past them without saying a word and got into the car. They both came to the car and asked me if I was all right and if I was able to get the sisters where they needed to go. I lied to the saint and her friend and told them I was fine and that, yes, the sisters all got to their apostolates. Monsignor said goodbye to Mother and got into the car. I waved goodbye to Mother.

As soon as we were off the property, Monsignor asked me what was wrong.

I said, "I just had the weirdest experience. Not one of the sisters knew where to go, so they told me they would ask their guardian angels to tell mine and for mine to tell me. They did, and he did. Somehow, I took them where they need to go, without a clue as to where I was going. It is really freaking me out."

Monsignor started to laugh. "O ye of little faith," he said. "Have you learned nothing from the sisters? They are the real deal. If they ask their angels to do something, their angels do it."

I learned thousands of lessons from Mother and her sisters. This one is extremely dear to me because now I have no need of GPS. My guardian angel always tells me where I need to be. In fact, sometimes my students test me because they know this story. When they do, I always tell them the same thing, "You pray the rosary, and I will ask my guardian angel to tell me how to get where we are going." What they do not realize is that this is really just the way my guardian angel and I get them to pray the rosary. Get to know your guardian angel who serves God by serving you.

CHAPTER THIRTEEN

Things to Avoid

THE SPIRITUAL LIFE IS OUR lives intertwined with the life of Christ. God created us for this relationship; thus, living it out will incur the wrath of the powers and principalities of darkness. They are against God and against everyone that is for God. As we live our lives with Christ, we must be on the lookout for warning signs of an attack. I do not say this to frighten you; I say this so that when you spot the signs, you can make the corrections necessary for keeping the demons at bay.

LOSING YOUR SENSE OF HUMOR

If you begin to notice that you have trouble laughing things off, it usually indicates falling into the trap of "woe is me." Victimhood drags us down and leads to systemic criticism and bitterness. Schisms, heresies, dissent, divisions, and irresolvable conflicts are all attitudes that reflect a loss of a sense of humor. Why? Because they all place greater importance on oneself and one's ideas. With a sense of humor, however, we can laugh about our situations and ourselves in a healthy way. It is the single character trait recommended by the saints. Life with Christ is serious, not sanguine, solemn, not somber. He is always on our side, wanting what is best for us in every situation and circumstance. Knowing and believing this (i.e., trusting him) enables us to see things clearly, to laugh when we should laugh and even to cry when we need to cry. Not to mention, the devil hates laughter.

PUT FEELINGS IN THEIR PLACE

It is far too easy to place undue importance on our feelings, whether positive or negative. Perceptions and feelings do have a role to play; after all, we are human beings, endowed with emotion and affect. We should neither cling to them nor outright reject them. The essence of prayer consists in the experience of faith, hope, and love. We do not feel these virtues. Sensory consolation or aridity is out of our hands. Sometimes, God grants us perceptions and feelings that inspire us and help us in times of weakness. We should be grateful for such times.

The absence of consolation, of feeling close to God, is really a sign that we are maturing, that our prayer is becoming purer, and that we are growing in faith, hope, and love for God. Numerous times, I heard Mother Teresa say that consolations are overrated. I understand now what she meant. We can become too dependent upon them and end up using our feelings as a barometer of our growth or lack thereof. Feelings do not determine the extent to which we are growing. We should be grateful whenever we feel the presence of the Lord, but faith transcends feelings. As St. Paul reminds us, we walk by faith and not by sight.

CHRISTIAN HOPE IS NOT OPTIMISM

Christian hope is not secular optimism because we base our hope on the promises of Christ and not the progress of man.

Resurrection after death, eternal life, and the certainty of God's love and grace in this life makes it possible for us to live through the most difficult and trying circumstances. We can confront the arduous conditions of life with dignity, and with grace, we can overcome moral evil and temptation in all its forms. It can be attractive to exchange hope for social or political progress, especially concerning those freedoms that men and women are searching for today. Yet we must remember that Christ never promised to eradicate in this life sickness, poverty, and other human dilemmas. However, he did tell us to respond to them. While we must strive to better the human condition as best we can, Christian hope is not a message of optimism for the future. Our destiny is eternal life. Our hope is to live forever in the loving communion we know as the Trinity. Secular expectations about a better future can never replace Christ, the true hope of the human race. Besides, most of the time, secular expectations and hopes are actually destructive.

Discouragement

Difficulties with forming the habit of prayer and a tendency toward perfectionism often lead a person to abandon prayer altogether. The desire is always for something hypothetically better, some abstract notion of what we imagine perfect prayer to be. In this life, we will never pray enough or be perfect enough in our prayer. That is what heaven is for!

Distractions are normal; aridity is normal; worries or preoccupations are normal. In fact, use them! If something comes to mind, instead of trying to push it away, talk to the Jesus about it. Yes, whatever it is. Most often, control over the conditions of our prayer is out of our hands. Physical illness, excessive heat or cold, and an inadequate place for praying may affect prayer, but you can make them a part of it. Abandoning prayer for better conditions or a more suitable frame of mind is wrong. Faith matures through not only perseverance, but by a persistence stimulated by love for God.

For example, "Lord my knee aches, and it is bothering me. I cannot concentrate on you. I know it aches because I am no longer young. I cannot do the things I used to do in the way I used to do them. I have to admit that I do not always like that I am aging. I know that means I am getting closer to you, but I guess I have some trepidation about dying. Maybe you can help me with this. Maybe my knee ache is actually my body groaning for my redemption. Maybe it is my body making a joyful noise unto you. I know I should be thinking about more lofty things, but it really does ache. Did you feel your body aging?"

Anything can become the content of prayer.

The Need for Effectiveness

Neither the experiences we have in prayer nor the results we see are the true measure of prayer's effectiveness. The efficacy comes from what God is undertaking in the depths of our soul. Here, we find the very source of our freedom and our faith, hope, and love. The times that we dedicate, perhaps incompetently, to prayer enable the Lord to be at work within us, facilitating an imperceptible growth. This can be frustrating. When we do not seem to be overcoming the characteristics of our temperament, deeply rooted impatience, impulsiveness, or sinful habits, we think prayer has no value. When we do not receive the things we ask for, we think prayer has no value.

Remember, prayer is not a means to an end. It is a means to communion with God. That alone should be enough for us. He will conform our minds and hearts to his Son. We need to trust that he is doing so. Prayer gives him the opportunity to be at work in the life of the believer and assures the Lord that we do indeed trust him. Sinful as I am, I make time for him each day. The alternative, not doing so, terrifies me. I know the only thing that God wants from me is me. Therefore, each day I go to him as I am, in whatever condition I am. Just give yourself to him, period.

SELF-SUFFICIENCY

You cannot do this alone. Every member of Christ's body needs help, including me. Self-sufficiency is demonic. Our prayer is always full of insecurities and illusions. Subtle temptations, deceptions, and confusion batter every one of us. We need the guidance of another, a spiritual director. We need someone competent, trained, and experienced to walk with us, a supportive and objective voice that keeps us on track and reassures us. We not only need to be inspired, but also need to be around people that pray, that make substantive time to be in conversation with the Lord. The lack of an atmosphere of prayer is contagious. Being in the company of the Lord's friends keeps us in company with the Lord.

I understand how difficult it is to find a spiritual director. The most important consideration in choosing one is not that the person is a priest. There are many consecrated women, many deacons and many laity that are competent and trained and experienced in spiritual direction. The person need not be a Catholic (although that is a definite plus). The person must be a devout Christian, someone that truly knows our Lord and understands how to lead a person closer to his heart. My spiritual director is not a Catholic priest. He is a retired Anglican bishop. It is as difficult for us priests to find a spiritual director as it is for you. Think outside the box and pray to the Holy Spirit to send one to you. You can meet by Skype, FaceTime, over the phone, email...

CHAPTER FOURTEEN

Conclusion

FAITH IS MUCH MORE THAN the sum total of everything we believe. Faith describes the stance we take before the world and the way in which we engage the world. Faith flows out of the belief that each one of us matters and that we exist to share God's life. In order to remain confident in this truth, we must allow Jesus to say this to us again and again and again. We must give the Lord the opportunity to affirm this truth and to express this truth in the unique conditions and circumstances of our existence. Prayer is the way we allow him to speak the words our hearts long to hear.

Christian prayer is, therefore, a lived ongoing conversation. It is a natural impulse of the will born of a humility that recognizes one's utter and complete dependence upon the gift of God's love. This impulse of the will is possible because baptism unites our lives with the life of Christ. Through this union with Christ, the Trinity moves into our lives with no intention of ever selling the house and moving away. God will never abandon us.

Prayer as an impulse of the will bursts forth in us both as an action of God and of ourselves, establishing a truly vibrant reciprocity. Through this mutual exchange of lives, we discover who we are and what the Lord longs to have us do for him and for others. We begin seeing God from a more intimate perspective, which transforms the way we see others, the world, and ourselves.

Therefore, we must take substantive time each day in solitude to commune with the Lord. Daily, we must open our hearts to his just as he took time to open his heart to the Father. The way of praying we learn from Jesus demands a purified heart, one that does not constantly dart about according to sentiments and emotions. Whether frustrated, anxious, arid, or on fire, our hearts must remain always fixed on God. We must acquire a heart like Our Lady's, open and receptive to whatever God requires, a heart completely trusting that the Lord will fulfill all his promises.

If we open ourselves to Mary, we can learn from her that fundamentally, prayer is an act of the will. Her vigilant heart enabled her to carry out everything the Lord asked of her, up to the moment of holding the bloodied body of her crucified Son. Even then, she willed to remain one with the God that had lifted her from her lowliness for exactly that moment. A heart that in the face of such horror and sorrow could nonetheless sing out from the depths of her sinless soul, "The Almighty has done great things for me and holy is his name."

Mary and every other saint, whether in heaven or on earth, carved out regular time each day to sit still in the presence of God. The secret to doing this lies in the recognition that we are nothing and that God is everything. This humility prevents us from falling into the temptation that our prayers are useless, that God does not hear us, and that we do not matter. The humility that enables us to speak heart-to-heart each day with the Lord assures us that we will live as we pray and pray as we live. It assures us that not only will God punctuate our day with signs of his presence, but also that we can punctuate his day with signs of our presence.

Jesus is sitting next to you right now, asking for a drink of water just as he asked the Samaritan woman so long ago. If you knew who it was that asks this of you, you would satiate his thirst by simply allowing him to love you. It truly is that simple.

ABOUT THE AUTHOR

Fr. Gary Caster was ordained in 1992 and is a priest of the Diocese of Peoria, Illinois. He has worked as a high school chaplain, religion teacher, and director of campus ministries at Bradley University, Eureka College, Illinois State University, and Illinois Wesleyan University. He worked with the office of family life to develop a program of marriage preparation, and taught Church history and ecclesiology to men in formation for the permanent diaconate. The author of several books, including *Joseph: The Man Who Raised Jesus, The Little Way of Lent: Meditations in the Spirit of St. Thérèse of Lisieux* and *The Little Way of Advent: Meditations in the Spirit of St. Thérèse of Lisieux*, Fr. Caster has also written and produced shows for EWTN. He is the Catholic chaplain at Williams College in Williamstown, Massachusetts, and leads retreats and parish missions.